ONE HUNDRED THIRTEEN MILLION
MARKETS OF
ONE

HOW THE NEW ECONOMIC ORDER
CAN REMAKE THE AMERICAN ECONOMY

CHRIS NORTON AND ROSS HONEYWILL

D0027869

Cover design by SPRING

Proof edited by Stephanie M. Clarke at StephanieMClarke.com

E book and print formatting by Dafeenah Jameel at IndieDesignz.com

All websites and information in this book are accurate at the time of publication.

ISBN: 978-0-9859134-0-3

Acknowledgements

All books are a collaborative effort, and this one is no exception. Thanks to Hazel Flynn for her patience in editing a book that was exploding in scope even as the deadlines loomed. Thanks also to Tracey Middleton for her input on the development of the modern consumer society and additional research into the companies whose stories are told in these pages.

Thanks also to Bryan Woolley for being the best possible sounding board for everything.

The biggest thanks of all go to our wives, Nicole and Greer, for giving us endless support and a reason for doing any of it.

Chapter Index

Chapter One- Hiding In Plain Sight 1

Chapter Two- The Better Way 13

Chapter Three- Welcome to the Two Planets 31

Chapter Four- The Earth Shifts Beneath Our Feet 39

Chapter Five- It's Not "The Economy, Stupid" 57

Chapter Six- Sliding Towards the Middle- The Starbucks Story 71

Chapter Seven- How to Out-NEO a NEO 87

Chapter Eight- Success and the Six-Hour Customer Call 101

Chapter Nine-"Worth It" 115

Chapter Ten- The Rules of the Global Economy, the Baked in Job and the Small Solution that Tackles the Big Problem 129

Chapter Eleven- The Next Great Economy 147

Chapter Twelve- The New Rules of the New Road 157

CHAPTER ONE
HIDING IN PLAIN SIGHT

There is a group of people in America powerful enough to act as the backbone on which we can rebuild our entire economy so that it can thrive in a globalized and technologically advanced world. Recently, there has been a heavy emphasis on the importance of "the one percent," a group that has come to be associated with wealth and power, but we aren't talking about them. Some of the group we are talking about are wealthy, but not all. Nor are they hedge fund traders, bankers, CEOs, social media entrepreneurs, celebrities, or any of the usual suspects assembled in a power line up. They are not bound by occupation, demographic, race, religion, gender, or political leaning. In fact they aren't even aware of the power they hold. They wouldn't even recognize one another in the street.

They are NEOs.

NEOs are the "New Economic Order." They have always been around but have come into their own over the last two decades. Their name comes from the fact that their spending adds up to an economy within an economy.

NEOs and the closely related Evolvers represent 46 percent of the U.S. adult population or 113 million people. Together their discretionary spending adds up to $3.8 trillion every year. That's around 77 percent of all discretionary consumer spending--every measure of the engine of true economic growth.

There are 59 million NEOs in America and 54 million Evolvers. They share many of the same values and psychological makeup but are differentiated by their levels of wealth, with Evolvers earning significantly less.

NEOs spend more money, more often than anyone else. They are credit crisis-proof, recession-proof, and they can make businesses that fit with their values recession-proof, too. Evolvers have to make more compromises but still aim to live by the same values when they can.

There are many things that make them stand out from the rest of the population. For example, NEOs and Evolvers are four times as likely to start a new business, and twice as likely to invest, or to graduate from college. They earn more, spend more, and do more than anyone else. They are repulsed by conspicuous consumption, and have a highly individualized view of the world, looking to express their own values through what they buy, what they do, and who they do it with.

Their discovery reveals that we are in the middle of a seismic shift in where the economic power lies in America. We just haven't had the ability to see them or the language to express it. Until now.

Amazingly, the economic significance of NEOs has remained largely misunderstood, thanks to our obsession with seeing people through the lens of "demographics:" income, education, race, gender or social, and political attitudes. All these ways of grouping people have useful information to tell us about them, but if you really want to understand the economic impact of one person or one group, you need to go straight to the bottom line and look at their spending.

If you're in a business of any size and ultimately rely upon someone somewhere to buy your product or service, then you need to know exactly who NEOs are and how they think. Doing so will give you a completely new understanding of what really drives different people to spend and help you engineer your business accordingly. Depending on the size and nature of your business, it's possible that you are spending millions in ways that will, at best, leave them cold and, at worst, drive them away. Knowing what they really value and what makes them tick will give you the tools to plot a far more fruitful path ahead, and expose vast areas of potential for those businesses that can offer the kind of high value goods and services they willingly pay for.

But you don't have to be in business to be interested in the New Economic Order. Whoever you are, their spending has already shaped the world in which you live and their values will continue to bring about profound social and economic change. Whether you are a political leader or simply someone who cares about the future of America, you may want to know more about why they are the backbone on which we can rebuild the American economy, particularly because it's a solution that allows us to move beyond the academic standoffs and political bickering that is contributing towards the current paralysis.

Or you might want to know where you fit into the new world we have discovered and what your contribution is.

There's no shortage of stories of companies, communities, and people slammed by globalization and, more recently, crushed by the Great Recession. Such stories and the human toll they represent are dreadful, but it's important to remember that there *are* other companies that are thriving, finding plenty of demand, and selling at prices far above their the rock bottom competitors.

In fact, the quest we embarked on that led to the discovery of NEOs was partly inspired by our inability to reconcile the kind of headlines that started to be tossed around after 2008. One minute we'd be told that all consumers were cutting back on spending across the board and the next minute someone would be talking about businesses achieving record growth or sales. That just didn't make sense.

Apple is one of the companies that hit the headlines for achieving record sales through the toughest economic times. Marketers explain its success by talking about great branding, engineers rhapsodize about the astounding engineering of its products, and demographers point towards the buying preferences of Gen X or Y. But each explanation throws up too many anomalies for it to fully account for Apples' success, or the success of many other business. After all, how do they account for Snooze?

Snooze is a breakfast joint that started in a slightly run down part of Denver in the last decade. The food is great, the staff quirky and fun, and the ambiance unique. Unlike Apple, Snooze doesn't have a global brand, runs virtually no advertising, and the closest thing to engineering it does is poaching and frying. Sit in any of their locations and you'll quickly see their customers are young, old, and everywhere in between; the demographics are all over the place! But you'll only discover this if you've been lucky enough to get a table in the first place.

Whatever the day of the week, there is likely to be a line out front. On weekends, it's a good idea to take breakfast with you so you have something to occupy your time while you wait in line for brunch. Each time Snooze opens a new location the same thing happens. All of these people, who seemed to be already well served with perfectly good breakfast joints, suddenly start lining up at the door for upside down pineapple pancakes, eggs benedict made with locally made mozzarella, and Noosa yogurt made with fresh cream from an enterprising (and seemingly lost) Australian in the nearby Rocky Mountains. But other places have great food. What makes Snooze different from the hundreds of restaurants, cafes and diners that go bust across America every week?

What about Anthropologie, the women's clothing and beauty retailer, whose stores are full of eclectic designs, vignettes, and personal shoppers? The company opened its first store in London in the worst economic period in decades, when companies were cutting back or closing down all around. Yet despite little or no fanfare and very little name recognition, women of all ages streamed in to the store, drawn by a sense of discovery and adventure. And they were more than happy to pay full retail price for the pleasure.

Mini, the small-car division of Germany's BMW, was expanding its network of urban Mini Stores all the way through the economic downturn that brought GM and Chrysler to their knees. Avery Brewing Company had to pull its White Rascal wheat beers and Ellie's Brown Ale out of many US states because it literally couldn't keep up with demand; meanwhile, Budweiser sales were shrinking, supposedly because of the bad economy.

And the list goes on. Steve Elis' Chipotle continues to take the fast food world by storm without a dollar menu. Chip Wilson's Lululemon opens one profitable store after another, selling yoga wear at twice the price brands as big as Nike charge. Zappos grows from nothing to over a billion dollars, selling shoes people can't try on before buying.

How can it be that companies as diverse as global technology behemoths, high-priced compact car makers, fast food outlets, women's clothing retailers, small time brewers, and an on-line catalogue can all find deep pockets of demand, when the evidence seems compelling that consumers "have no money to spend, are holding back on purchases and only looking for discounts and value?"

We decided to look beyond these companies and their individual business talents, products, and services and instead concentrate on the one thing that binds this seemingly disparate group together: their customers. When we looked, we discovered that they were NEOs and Evolvers.

Before we tell you who they are, however, we need to tell you who they aren't. Some of these NEOs are young, but by no means all. Some of them are creative, but they may just as easily be accountants or doctors. Some have kids (or grandkids) but others couldn't take care of a houseplant. They are not Yuppies, Dinks, Boomers, Generation X-ers, The Creative Class, Outliers, or any of the other labels we so readily throw around.

These labels do have a use. They can tell us some things about the people who fall into their categories. But they tell us nothing about the only thing that really matters economically – how they spend.

Understand NEOs and Evolvers and they have the power to rock your world.

The Big Issues

The discovery of NEOs was astonishing and exciting, only dwarfed by the realization that not only had we revealed an entire economy within an economy, but we had uncovered a major shift in the power base of America *and* stumbled upon the key to immediate and sustainable economic growth for the country.

When it comes to looking at who holds the power in America today, we have been looking in the wrong direction. We have been seduced by the idea that it is held by the one percent, or those with the most wealth. We aren't going to say that there isn't a link between money and power. But discretionary spending is the engine that drives the economy. The New York media might be titillated by the number of Porsches hedge fund traders are buying, but it's not really significant in a $15 trillion economy. So, in terms of who has continued to power the economy throughout the toughest times in living memory, we have to look at the issue from the other direction, at those who are responsible for 77 percent of consumer spending and most of the profit that businesses' make: NEOs and Evolvers.

How could this have slipped anyone's notice? It's long been assumed that there is a link between wealth and spending. It seems common sense to think that the more you have, the more you spend and, conversely, the less you have, the more you hang on to what you've got. Yet the same research that allowed us to discover the existence of NEOs and Evolvers also showed that they spend more money, more frequently than the rest of the population. To a great extent, it's that spending that makes them such a powerful force, one that has shaped the world in which we live and one that points to them being the backbone on which we can rebuild the entire economy.

At least everyone can agree we need to do that. With stubbornly high unemployment, the prospects of ongoing slow growth and crushing budget deficits, the U.S. is currently experiencing economic and political paralysis.

Big problems inevitably invite big solutions. President Obama called for a modern day "Sputnik Moment." In the age of the iPad, Internet, and Cloud computing it's common to look for large technological jumps to come to the rescue of economies. Whether it is at MIT, Silicon Valley, or a private research facility, there is always a technological development underway that "has the potential to change our society." But betting on it turning up at just the right time *and* delivering the boost to the economy that we need, to boot, is a huge gamble.

Simply put, we can challenge the prevailing wisdom about where the potential for growth in our economy is. We can produce high value new jobs and new stellar companies in areas where others see only consolidation and decline. And we can do this because the demand is there, if you know what to look at.

Can it really be as simple as that? After years of high spending everyone "knows" we are all up to our eyeballs in debt, terrified of the future, and convinced our best days are behind us. Economists tell us that the economy is sluggish because these factors mean that there is no demand. In fact some days it seems remarkable that we have any economy left at all.

Yet we have already listed a number of companies that have enjoyed a high level of demand that has allowed them to achieve an extraordinary level of success.

When we discovered these successes are driven by NEOs and Evolvers, we realized that there is still a long way to go in terms of providing the kind of goods and services that they value. As you come to learn more about NEOs and Evolvers, you will see the hallmarks of their preferences all around you, and you will also see there is enormous scope for development in the NEO economy. You'll be able to spot growth opportunities where others see none in sectors ranging from banking and baking to pharmacy and farming.

Given the right mix of factors, price is rarely the key factor in their buying choices, so being the lowest cost producer isn't the only way to succeed in the NEO economy. That means that growing it can fill the gaps left by all those lower cost producers in China and elsewhere.

Businesses have invested millions in understanding their customers, so if what we are saying is true, how can it be that this powerful group has remained virtually invisible?

Businesses do have more stored data about our actions and preferences than ever before. But their data may just as well be astrology charts for all the protection it gives them. This even applies to the most data-driven company in the world--Google--a company created and run by seriously smart people who make the vast majority of their revenue selling advertising space to people who want the inside track. In 2011, that revenue added up to nearly $40 billion. Impressive stuff.

But take a moment and look at the ads on your browser or favorite web page. How many of them are even remotely interesting to you? Many? Any? How many have you actually *acted* on? If one of the most innovative companies on the planet, which knows more about your online behavior than anyone else, can't predict what you want with any real accuracy, then you'd be forgiven for thinking it can't be done. You'd be forgiven, but you'd still be wrong.

It took someone like Steve Jobs, who railed against focus groups and famously said that "...people don't know what they want until you show it to them," to create the iMac/iPod/iPhone/iPad. And it took Starbucks' Howard Schulz to go against every piece of advice business experts gave him and open up an espresso bar in the corner of a retail store during a massive recession. Or the people at Snooze to open a breakfast joint in the middle of a town full of breakfast joints where everyone seems to have a wheat or dairy allergy!

Where does this 'magical demand' come from? Is it just an overnight mass shift in consumption patterns, or is it simpler than that? When you focus on the consumers and not the companies, a very different picture emerges.

It takes a fundamental shift in understanding to see where the real opportunities are in America today. The good news is that we haven't even scratched the surface of its potential.

The NEO economy is thriving and still has much, much room for more. Understand the new rules of the road and endless vistas of business and opportunity open up.

A New Model for Growth

We all understand the devastation brought about by large scale offshoring of jobs that were once the backbone of our smokestack cities even as we simultaneously search on-line for the lowest price flat screen TVs manufactured in China. But we are missing a major part of the puzzle if we see this as simply a battle between the emerging economies of the world and American workers and businesses. Much more is going on, and we can see it when we look at the bigger picture.

Go back just 40 years and nobody talked about having "a relationship with their bank's brand" (if they'd thought about it at all, they would seen bank brand as simply its name and letterhead), but almost everyone knew their local bank manager and he knew them. He was a real live human person, who had the time and authority to get to know your personal situation before deciding if you could have a loan.

That seems quaint in a world where people have been replaced by policies and the distance between the company and the customer feels too wide to be broached. The kind of automation that means you can be pushed through a series of options that don't fit the reason you're calling before being dumped out without getting to speak to anyone, or moving the "contact center" to India seems like a good decision when you don't have any real contact with the customer in the first place. Little wonder that we feel like commodities, shipped about like any other by the banks, even though we are the ones who are keeping them solvent.

Our food is now produced in factories miles away from us (often in other countries), sold by massive retailers who answer to shareholders over local communities. Doctors have gone from being part of our lives from cradle to grave, to part of a system that can boot us out at will. The list goes on and on.

There is plenty of upside to the changes that have taken place over the last 50 years, such as cheaper food, bigger capital markets, and endless advances in medical treatments. The thirst for efficiency in all that we do has allowed companies to lower costs, reduce waste, and expand their reach. These measures have expanded our economy many times over, creating massive wealth along the way and established American businesses at the heads of almost every category across the world.

But as we continue to chew our way to the bottom line we have started to consume ourselves. Few can win in the race to the bottom.

The discovery of the NEO economy shows that it is economically profitable to create new goods and services which will appeal to people who are delighted to buy them. It reveals a positive loop of growth that offers opportunity for all.

It isn't trickle-down economics, where the money held by a few is supposed to benefit the many. This is drive-it-forward, make-it-better, and give-people-what-they-want economics. And it certainly isn't an economy built on accelerated consumption, where people buy more stuff that they neither want nor need that gets shoved to into the garage before being relegated to the piles of other stuff accumulating in storage facilities across the country.

The list of businesses that NEOs and Evolvers have made successful is long and impressive, but when you understand what they value and are willing to pay more for, you can see that there is scope for someone to create the Zappos of banks, one that sees its customers as financial partners for life rather than having to bribe them with their own cash back to stay.

There is the potential for a 'Lululemon of telecommunications' company that has almost no churn because its customers know they will always provide the ideal solution rather than spending a fortune getting through to a human being and asking plaintively, "Can you hear me now?"

You will see that there are millions of customers eager and willing to pay higher costs to green power companies so they don't have to be shoving against Big Oil at the trough of government subsidies.

The discovery of NEOs and Evolvers points towards thousands of new business opportunities, of all sizes, in all sectors, and the jobs they create capable of providing the way of life we want here in America.

An extra one percent of GDP, year after year, derived from increased spending by those with the highest propensity and ability to spend, on top of the economic growth already forecast, turns a slumbering economy into a booming one, shrinks unemployment and allows us to grow out of our debt challenges.

Put simply, a three percent increase in spending by NEOs and Evolvers can lead to a permanent increase in the United States' GDP of one percent. It's even possible that a spending increase of less than three percent can bring about the same growth in GDP as the multiplier effect of every dollar spent in the NEO Economy is much greater.

This is the promise of the NEOs and the potential of the NEO Economy.

Our understanding of NEOs is based on the scientific study of more than a million people on three continents over 10 years. It challenges much "received wisdom" and so will be hard for some people to accept. Of course about 113 million of you will be quietly saying to yourself "I knew this all along." Now you have the facts to prove it.

NEOs are already influencing our society in a myriad of ways, but so far they've been hiding in plain sight. You're about to get the key that will enable you to spot NEOs wherever they may be. You'll learn the language of NEOs and Evolvers and their counterparts: High Status Traditionals and Traditionals (for the sake of simplicity, we'll refer to them as NEOs and Traditionals unless we need to make a distinction that specifically relates to Evolvers and High Status Traditionals).

You'll see what has shaped the world as it is today and, more importantly, how it can be shaped tomorrow.

If you're in business, NEOs *are* the highly sought after 'high value' customers you've been looking for, and it's worth going back to the drawing board and seeing how you can renegotiate the terms of your contract with them.

If you are a NEO or an Evolver, you'll see how you fit into the bigger picture and how you are the future of the American economy, just by being who you are.

And if you are the President of the United States, you probably want to pay attention, because the NEO Economy is the power pump that will turn this country around and solve the financial problems it has dug itself into.

But we are getting ahead of ourselves. First, you need to understand what makes NEOs and Evolvers so radically different from the rest of society and what they really value.

Let's get started.

CHAPTER TWO
THE BETTER WAY

"So who are these people, then?"

We were sitting in one of our favorite bakeries grabbing something to eat after yet another meeting with a client to discuss their customer base. It doesn't really matter now who it was but if it were real estate we probably talked about Baby Boomers and Empty Nesters, whereas for telecommunications the conversations would have been about "Principled Professionals" or "Work Hard, Play Hard," or some such terminology.

Most of the companies we dealt with, and those we didn't, divided their customer base, both current and targeted, in to smaller and smaller segments to try to produce offerings that more closely match their perceived desires. Some used language that began in Marketing and passed in to general usage, such as "Gen X-er" or "High Net Wealth Individual." Others paid fortunes to develop their own segmentation in the belief it gave them a competitive advantage. Whatever the level of sophistication, it basically came down to a relatively simple formula: a few key characteristics, such as age, income, zip code, or past level of purchase (and, for those with bigger budgets, psychographics thrown in) crunched to reveal who was likely to buy what.

But sitting in this individually owned bakery, stuffed to capacity with people eating handmade sandwiches on Russian Rye or Rustic French bread made just out of our eye line, we couldn't help thinking about who were these people who were happy to pay a significant premium to eat food that they could have had more quickly and more cheaply at any one of the branded places within the surrounding blocks.

"Urban sophisticates" said one of my colleagues, Paul, as a dollop of cilantro mayonnaise dripped on to his shirt.

"Yuppies" said another, called Karen.

"Foodies" said a third.

"Trust fund babies with nothing better to do with their time than sit around and worry about whether the chicken they are eating died happy." Said the stern young intern, overlooking the fact that we, too, were regular customers and that description didn't fit us at all.

But as we looked around the only real conclusion that you could draw was that whatever label we could come up with, there was someone else who could just as easily be fitted in to a completely opposite category. There were young mothers cooing over their offspring, and businessmen talking about start-ups and venture capital. For each "urban sophisticate" there seemed to be a fair few "suburban un-sophisticates," and so on.

"O.k., let's just assume that they are all Foodies," I said. After all food was the one common element we could at least observe. "What happens when they leave this place?"

"What do you mean?"

"Well, in here we are all Foodies, but then we walk in to a bank and we are a host of other things. We become "Heads of Families," "700 plus credit scores," "Savers," etc. etc. Do we stop being Foodies then? What about when it comes to watching TV tonight? Does the fact that I love the homemade apple and blackberry pie in here have any relevance to which shows I choose to watch, or how likely I am to buy any of the products that are advertised to me during those shows?"

"Well that depends on a whole range of factors" said Paul. "It depends on what generation you are from, how much education you have, what stage of life you are at, and whether you are a 'go getter' or not."

"I don't have a TV," said Karen. "Used to. But I never seemed to watch it. So I got rid of it."

"If Paul's right and those are the real drivers," I was thinking aloud. "That should mean behavior is fairly predictable. They're fairly measurable, after all. Then why does so much of what people spend money on not fit in to any of those patterns? We all have college degrees, we're high earners, most of us are home owners, and if we weren't "go getters", we wouldn't have made it this far, but when I asked where we should go for lunch, we had suggestions of everything from McDonald's, to a high-end chain steakhouse, to this place. So I have to question how much of an indicator of spending all of those factors really are, even if only on lunch?"

"Most of the models out there are based on what people are doing right now. Maybe the really useful thing would be to be able to know what someone is going to do next." Said Charles, by far the most intelligent of all of us, and by no coincidence the one who tended to speak less and say more.

As often happened after Charles offered an opinion, silence descended upon the group. His brief comment had touched on something that had been troubling me for many years. Business had become increasingly more complex in the way that they divided up customers. Ever greater amounts of data were being used to produce reams of "consumer understanding." But the harsh truth was that they hadn't really become that much better at it.

Time after time I would sit in meetings with the people who built the products or developed the services and who could talk with almost complete accuracy about what things would cost, when they would be delivered, and the impact upon everything of one small part of the design, development, and production value chain. It was all mightily impressive. But when we talked about the small matter of revenue (the part of the business that paid everyone's wages), despite the increase in 'metrics around marketing response, brand value, sales performance,' and so on, it was blindingly obvious that we had departed the realms of science and entered some version of projection, speculation, irrelevancy or, in many cases, purebred bullshit.

Virtually every way of describing consumer behavior seemed to involve "shoehorning" conclusions to fit whatever model was being used in an approach that barely differed from the everyday in its sophistry. In fact, every day one expert or another made statements along the lines of "everyone" is eating cupcakes now," completely excluding everyone that isn't!

Many bestsellers are based on models that only work if you ignore the evidence that doesn't fit. *Trading Up: Why Consumers Want New Luxury Goods—and How Companies Create Them* by Michael Silverstein, Neil Fiske, and John Butman is a good example. In the introduction to the paperback edition, Silverstein, a partner at Boston Consulting Group, writes, 'We conducted a large-scale, quantitative survey of consumers in China…Consumers there have experienced tremendous growth in personal income and have enough discretionary wealth that they are beginning to spend on premium goods and services that they believe will help them fulfill their dreams.' Undoubtedly there is a great deal of evidence to support this conclusion and BCG are an excellent firm, but at the same time it totally negates and ignores the hundreds of millions of Chinese who follow more traditional ways (thrift, investing in real estate, etc.) and are spectacularly uninterested in expensive premium goods and services, even those who are acquiring wealth at exactly the same rate as the identified spenders. If they don't fit the narrative, they apparently just disappear.

It occurred to some of us around that lunch table that there might be far more useful information buried in the offcuts—all those inconvenient facts that had been cast aside to create these supposedly foolproof models of what made consumers tick.

The first thing we had to do was to test the widespread assumptions about demographics, education level, occupation, and income. Were they as important as we have been told for so long?

It's so obvious it doesn't need noting that there are differences between people even if they are part of the same generation, have similar income levels or fit in to any of the other psycho-graphic identity labels. And we aren't talking incremental differences here; we're talking about the level of difference there is between a hamster and an asteroid.

We also had to test the 'truths' about the high-end and low-end of the market. It's always been assumed self-evident that 'people with money and taste' would buy beautiful, discretionary products, and experiences, whilst those on low incomes would only spend on the staples. This is the basis of virtually every economic model of consumer spending and leads to recipes for economic recovery (depending upon who you are listening to) that involve putting more money in the hands of the rich, the middle class, or the poor, who will then spend in a highly predictable manner based upon the amount of money they have in their bank account.

In the real world, consumer behaviors differ wildly. Some people are buying Windows laptops while others are passionate about Apple products and there is little chance of dragging either of them across to 'the other side'. Some are looking for comfort in crowds and are orientated primarily by brands or celebrity, while others are striking out on the path less travelled, even if it is just in the preserves they spread on their toast in the morning. Many are looking only for the best price or an unbeatable deal while others are looking for the best experience at almost any price. Anecdotally, we could see that knowing someone's income, age, or education level wouldn't tell you which is which, but if we were going to butcher one of the most sacred cows of business, we figured we might want a little more than anecdotes!

It was becoming crystal clear that if we were going to be able to figure out why consumers made the choices they made, we'd need to be able to explain the whole picture, not just the parts that fit. We needed a better model.

A New Perspective

"A good hockey player skates to the puck, a great hockey player skates to where it is going to be." Wayne Gretzky

Having decided to pay attention to our nagging concerns about the models used, we wanted to add something significant to the understanding of consumer behavior. Something that businesses could actually use and that would add value. Rather than just track what consumers had done in the past (where the puck is), we had to be able to explain why they did it so that we could predict what they were going to do in the future (where the puck is going to be).

We realized that to get a clear and complete picture we had to use completely independent data and test that data on our own dime rather than submit ourselves to the pressure of pleasing clients. Accessing hundreds of thousands of survey respondents, we were able to put together more than two billion points of data, from an impeccable, independent, single source, Roy Morgan Research, collecting information on three continents, including the U.S.A.

We hoped there would be, at most, four or five different social segments that fell out of our analysis. Anything larger than that is useful only in theory. It can never be operationalized in order to make any real difference. We'd sat through far too many business discussions dividing different types of consumers into ever smaller groups, only to see them all merged back in to the same old sausage machine when it came to execution. We wanted something that businesses could put to work.

Putting Spending Center Stage

As there were already numerous approaches that grouped people according to demographic factors, such as age or gender, we decided to put these to one side. We centered our new model around discretionary spending. Discretionary spending is that sum of money you've got left after you've paid your rent and covered other essentials, the sum you can spend as you choose, whether that be on going to a restaurant or buying a set of line skates. It's the part of the economy that rises and falls most with the trade cycle, influencing whether businesses succeed or fail in the process and in so doing, impacting the economy as a whole. Having done that, we set out to examine behaviors and attitudes, always looking for the significant factors that discriminated the most between consumer choices. We weren't interested in what made consumers similar, only what made them significantly different.

Even toying with the idea that whether someone was Generation X or Y couldn't really tell us anything reliable about their spending is heresy enough in some circles, but we had to identify those things that really mattered when it came to people's spending behavior. They weren't always the things that people initially thought mattered. For example, 92 percent of Americans declared themselves to be proudly American. But by digging deeper into the factors they used to make real decisions (using analysis of variance or ANOVA), national pride soon bit the dust as a significant spending factor.

This was complex modeling with thousands of behaviors, values, and attitudes used as inputs, then correlated to multiple measures of spending.

The results were startling.

We were able to analyze individual choices and factors to look at the impact of age, education, income, and wealth. These were the cornerstones of consumer and economic theory but the results showed that none of these factors was actually statistically significant in predicting an individual's propensity to spend, nor in predicting what they would choose to buy when they did.

We were excited by what we found, but we had to be sure. So we ran the analyses again and again.

Each time, the results were consistent. They showed that the factors used to make economic and business decisions every day were of no significant relevance when it came to predicting what people would do next, or where the puck was going.

When it came to wealth, money is, of course, a significant factor in spending (people had to be able to afford something in order to buy it), but simply having the money to buy something wasn't the determining factor. In fact, it was a very poor indicator of whether a specific person would buy a specific product. Indeed, lots of people with lots of money have no intention of spending it at all.

The same was true of age and other demographic breakdowns. You have only to look to see that a Baby Boomer architect from San Francisco has little in common with a truck driving Baby Boomer from La Crosse, Minnesota, yet businesses of all sizes insist on acting as if they do. Now we had the proof that someone's "date of manufacture" has very little impact upon why and how they spend money.

For anyone schooled and drilled in the idea that demographic factors are the key influence when it comes to spending, this discovery is shocking enough. After all, it's the backbone of many multi million dollar marketing campaigns and the bedrock of many economic policies. But we weren't finished.

Although these factors didn't serve as useful guides to spending by themselves, perhaps they worked best in combination? We had to test whether a mix of age and income and education X and Y produced a more accurate result. We ran the data and once again it was a firm no.

Combining sex and age group, with hobbies, with income, with geographic location, and on and on, gave the impression that a business was effectively identifying its customers and building a clearer picture of them, but as we delved deeper, we found that none of these factors is what really drives spending. In fact, the picture only got more opaque as more irrelevancies were added.

In short, irrelevant x irrelevant did **not** = relevant!

Demographics do have a use. Knowing how many people there are in different age groups, and what their income levels are, is vital if you're planning government services or age-correlated products like healthcare. But what demographics don't tell you is how likely someone is to spend money. And if they are spending money on lunch, it won't tell you if they're more likely to go to McDonald's or a local bakery.

This explained to us why there were so many anomalies, both in the bakery crowd we'd noticed and in society in general.

If we are going to be rational (and we are) we have to be prepared to accept that when the results do not fit our model, it is not the results that are wrong, it's our original model that was at fault. We don't just get to ignore the bits that don't fit our existing conclusions.

So, if wealth and demographics such as gender, education, and so on are such poor indicators of where the puck was going, what *could* tell us?

We began by considering three core variables:

1. Behavior

The first is the simple one of behavior; what people actually do. This is the one that most predictive models are based upon, as in "people who bought this book also bought this one too…" The problem with behavior is that it can change in a heartbeat. No matter that you have been eating Heinz ketchup for 20 years, if you one day taste the 365 brand from Wholefoods and discover that it tastes much better, you may change your behavior on the spot, switching ketchup allegiance in a moment. Behavior tells us where the puck is, not necessarily where it is going. Understand this and it becomes clear that most predictive models, such as the ones used to value both online and offline advertising, are simply a combination of mostly irrelevant attributes (age, sex, income, etc.) and past behaviors. Perhaps they're better than nothing, but not much.

2. Attitudes

The second element in our model was attitudes. Attitudes tend to change slowly over time, as opposed to highly volatile behavior, but what is their relevance to spending? Was there a positive correlation between say social, religious, political or any other distinct views and the outcome of spending in the real world? Were, for example, attitudes towards gun rights, gay marriage, the death penalty, or immigration in any way correlated to whether someone was a potential high value consumer? How do attitudes drive spending?

3. Values

The third, and most stable element of our working model, was values. Values tend to change very, very slowly, often over generations. While attitudes to issues such as minority rights can change typically within years or often decades, values typically change only over generations. For example an immigrant family from Latin America may value their Catholic religion as a core part of their identity and raise their children in primarily the same way they were raised. Their children, in turn, may do mostly the same with their offspring, and so on. Whether we explicitly articulate them or not, we tend to hold on to our personal values a lot more closely than we do our ketchup brand preference.

The question we were asking was a big one. When it comes to spending, what is the predictive power and relative importance of values, attitudes, and behaviors? Nobody had ever been able to answer this before.

As we continued our analysis what we saw emerging was nothing less than amazing, a career-changing moment, challenging everything we thought we knew.

There were 10 discretionary spending factors, 82 attitudinal/value factors and no less than 100 behavioral factors, or characteristics, that could be crunched to pinpoint those consumers among the mass who were fans of organic baking and cutting edge technology, who had a thirst for individualism, and spent their money accordingly. What we saw was so contradictory to all the other expert wisdom out there we simply didn't believe it at first.

So, we set new parameters that stripped out all but the consumers in the top 25 percent of discretionary spending and the top 40 percent of discriminating behaviors and attitudes. This was surely going to crash the model and send us scuttling back to the demographers and consumer segmentors, tail between our legs.

We ran the data again and again and each time out came the same result. We had clearly identified high-spending individuals who showed an interest in such things as design, uniqueness, and authenticity--and not just a few of them. We were looking at 59 million Americans, a nation within the nation. At 24 percent of the adult population they accounted for more than half of all discretionary spending in the economy. Further analysis showed that 92 percent of them were in what is known as the Big Spender category, that is, the top third of discretionary spenders. So powerful was their influence that we began to refer to them as the New Economic Order, or NEOs.

As well as the NEOs, there was another group, 22 percent of the population, who shared most of the NEOs' defining values, attitudes, and behaviors but lacked the financial capacity to spend enough to qualify them for this top group. All it would take to push them over the line was an increase in income, and so we began to call them Evolvers (for Evolving NEOs). They were like NEOs in almost every way--they just lacked some of the funds, so didn't get to express their NEO characteristics as consistently.

Together, NEOs and Evolvers numbered 113 million American--an entirely separate NEO Economy.

So what of everyone else? The largest group of non-NEOs consisted of 120 million people or around 52 percent of adults, who amazingly accounted for only 23 percent of discretionary spending. When it came to spending, they were attracted to a combination of status, features, price, and deals, making them almost the reverse of the NEOs. Only four percent of them were in the big spender category.

Yet when we looked at them, many earned fat salaries or were wealthy; they just didn't particularly like spending their money, and when they did they had to feel that they were getting an extraordinary deal. As these people basically fit the model of consumers we've all been force fed over the last 50 years, we called them Traditionals.

Within the large group of Traditionals, some did spend more than others (although in a totally different way to their NEO counterparts). These we called High Status Traditionals, because of their fondness for high status goods. This was a real 'Aha!' moment for us, because at once we could understand the dichotomy of the high status wealthy which the luxury goods industry and glossy lifestyle media are so focused upon. It made sense that if you gave some young rap artists, sports stars, or Wall Street Traders, rapidly incremental wealth, many of them would immediately spend wildly on the conspicuous consumption of large houses, big cars, and obvious jewelry. That is exactly what High Status Traditionals do. It was remarkably predictable. We'd be lying if we said we didn't smile at the thought of Donald Trump and 50 Cent being in the same category.

As exciting as this was, it was our next discovery that was crucial in figuring out how to reach NEOs. As we repeated the studies and analysis of this wealth of data we found that being able to *accurately* identify the reasons for consumer spending challenged all sorts of other accepted wisdom. Notably, the commonly held view is that consumers are in a constant state of flux, blown this way and that by economic circumstance, marketing, star power, and a thousand other variables or trends.

Instead, what we saw was a picture of extraordinary consistency. This is not saying that what people spent their money on over time didn't change, but the core values on which they made those decisions certainly did not. Again, there are critical differences between NEOs and Traditionals. Traditionals' spending tended to mirror external factors, such as perceptions of the economy as a whole, so that it rises in periods of perceived economic prosperity and falls in periods of recession or threat (hello, Great Recession). The spending of the NEOs is far more consistent. NEOs spend money on the things that match their values throughout the booms *and* the busts. If they do cut back, it tends to be on products with which they had a far weaker personal values match.

Suddenly we started to ask a whole range of new questions. Could the NEO Economy be resistant to the peaks and valleys of consumer confidence in a way we've been told is impossible? Did this explain why certain companies flourished during the periods after 9/11 and during the recession while others, who superficially appeared to have the same attributes, had been pounded by the "bad economy"? Was it really about the customers that these companies attracted and their values, rather than the economy at large or the individual company? Was this all far more predictable, and therefore usable, than the picture of constantly changing consumer trends had trained us to believe?

As we continued to develop our discoveries, the global audit and accounting giant KPMG took an interest and conducted a forensic independent evaluation of our model, comparing it to standard U.S. research models like Yankelovich. They declared it the most robust and usable model available.

We had indeed struck gold. We'd arrived at a rigorous way of modeling that closed the gaps in what had previously seemed like anomalies in consumer behavior. But this is science, not ideology, so we ran the model time after time to ensure it remained both robust and predictive. We found the only necessary changes to keep the model current concerned behaviors. In the earliest data, the willingness to use telephone banking was a discriminator, separating NEOs from Traditionals. But as time passed and technology developed, it lost its usefulness, to be replaced by Internet banking and, more recently, mobile banking. This kind of adjustment was, however, tinkering at the margin. The model itself proved astoundingly strong and predictive.

What we had established through this exhaustive process was that there are two comprehensively different types of consumers in the economy, two vastly different types of people in society. So different it's as if they may as well be from different planets.

We had found a better way.

We had identified the top third of discretionary spenders in the economy and found what made them totally distinct from their Traditional counterparts.

But it wasn't until we shifted our own focus that the real revelation hit home. Until then, we had viewed consumers through the eyes of businesses and corporations. We had divided consumers into groups and thought about ways in which they could be targeted and their perceptions and opinion shaped and changed.

Suddenly, we were able to step into the shoes of NEOs, Evolvers, High Status Traditionals, and Traditionals and see how businesses and corporations appeared to them. That was the real revelation—the one that allowed us to reconcile the anomalies, close the gaps, resolve the contradictions, and understand exactly why some businesses were succeeding and others were struggling.

Put simply these insights were:

1. *Individual consumer behavior is incredibly consistent*-- Switching between views of consistently NEO behavior and consistently Traditional behavior seems confusing until you have the language to distinguish them. We had discovered that there *were* no anomalies, no offcuts. Each person behaves almost perfectly according to type.

The longitudinal research showed that individual traits do not change over time; that the distinct attitudes that define someone as either being NEO or Traditional do not alter in relation to changes in their discretionary wealth. Give a Traditional $1 million and they don't start behaving like a NEO. They either behave like a High Status Traditional or carry on exactly as they did before they had the money. Give an Evolver $1 million and they don't start spending like a High Status Traditional. In fact over 10 years of data, not one person switched from one side of the divide to the other!

By truly understanding the motivations behind individual spending decisions, many things became much clearer. It explained concepts such as *The Millionaire Next Door*, the story of someone who, through thrift, has been able to accumulate significant assets but feels no need to express them through spending. Clearly this person is a Traditional who, despite their wealth, continues to make all of their spending decisions through the matrix of price, features, and--to a far lesser extent--status (although *not* spending money can clearly become a status symbol to some).

It also explained something else that we were beginning to see more and more. The news was beginning to report that "consumers were cutting

25

back on spending across the board" at the same time as they talked about "…record iPad sales," or, "Consumers seeking deals on cars," and "Five month waitlist for Audi S5."

It wasn't the case at all that all consumers were doing anything. A convergence of factors that we will go on to talk about, were causing the two groups we had identified to polarize.

2. *NEOs and Traditionals behave the same around commodities*-- NEOs only begin to act like NEOs when they find products or services that are a reflection of their distinctive values. If price or features are the only distinguishing factors, whether it is a product or service, it is effectively a commodity and NEOs and Traditionals behave in entirely the same way. Many of our artisan bread buyers were more than willing to jump from one telecom provider to another for a better price or a new phone, but try to get them to give up an iMac for a PC, or fresh baked rye for Wonder Bread and they'd look at you in disbelief. This sowed the seed for us to start looking at areas of the economy that have become less individual, more commoditized over time, for opportunities of economic differentiation. If NEOs and Evolvers spend to their potential with companies with whom they feel an affinity, how could we profoundly increase the level of this connection to drive long term, high value economic growth?

3. *NEO and Traditionals' spending is so distinct that you could effectively see them as coming from two very different planets*--It was the stark differences and distinctions between these two groups that led us to exclaim that it was like looking at the denizens of two different planets – Planet NEO and Planet Traditional.

Applying the understanding that consumers effectively came from two different planets made us look at the world in an entirely different way. Over on Planet NEO, NEOs and Evolvers made those businesses with a product or service that is extraordinary and truly unique successful.Over on Planet Traditional, Traditionals frequented those businesses that arrived at the right combination of price, features, and status. But the vast majority of businesses were caught in the vacuum between those two planets, neither appealing to the innate drivers of NEOs nor the economic thirst of Traditionals. This is bad enough at any time, but when the economy hit the skids in 2008, it proved to be deadly. There is no life in a vacuum, so businesses drifting in this space are eventually doomed.

4. *Given that consumers are consistent, our ability to understand and align with what drives them determines our likelihood of economic success*--Our research showed that most of the factors that had been believed to exert the greatest influence on spending had very limited impact in reality. It also suggested an entirely different explanation for the success--or failure--of many businesses.

As we delved more, it certainly explained the fluctuating fortunes of Apple, a story that we will retell in the light of this new information in chapter five, and other businesses, whose stories you will also find in this book. For now, rather than seeing Apple as having created a market, it becomes clear that the company's fluctuations in fortunes en route to its current success are due to the degree to which it was in alignment with what NEOs want and are willing to pay for. Apple will continue to lead the field as long as it continues to meet NEOs on their own planet and up until another technology company outflanks it.

Of course, millions of companies survive which are clearly neither the Extraordinary nor the Extraordinary deal, but in a globalized world with a relentless push towards commoditization, just good enough is no longer going to be good enough. Merely surviving is not sustainable. The next round of globalization or technological improvement could be the one that takes you down.

And, as discretionary spending is key to economic growth, it is no great leap to say that it isn't just individual businesses that succeed when they are in alignment with what unlocks consumer spending. It's our entire economy.

Why do we use the word 'alignment?' The 'one world' view, based on the idea that all consumers are the same, assumes that they are there to be persuaded or won over, or divided by offers, brand qualities and advertising. The revelation that there are actually Two Planets, however, and the consistency of consumers revealed by our research flips the power base of the relationship and says, if you are in business, rather than winning consumers over, you will succeed or fail in direct relationship to how closely you can mirror what either planet values in your offering. The NEOs are there – but do you know how to unlock their spending in the way that Apple does?

5. *If consumers are consistent, businesses can be more dynamic*--Businesses new and old can actively and consciously engineer themselves from nose to tail to increase their alignment with either of the two consumer planets. In other words, when you know what unlocks the spending behavior of either group, you can do more of what works and drop what doesn't or what isn't necessary. Discovering what consumers really value opens up opportunities for huge efficiencies as less time and money is spent on developing, engineering and marketing products to people who are either unlikely to value them or in many cases like them but would be unwilling to pay for them.

We had achieved what we had set out to do. We had delved deeper into consumer behavior and discovered something that enabled us to develop a model that businesses could use in everything from deciding on their advertising and marketing strategy to developing new products and services.

But more than that, although we didn't fully comprehend it at the time, we had discovered what could become the foundations of a plan for economic revival, right here in our own backyard.

Over on Planet Traditional, most businesses compete on price and brand. If we look to build our economy solely upon the demand for goods and services predominantly competing on price, it necessarily puts every company and job in competition with technology and factories and workers in all four corners of the world. We are building hundreds of jobs in marketing agencies but losing millions in making the products.

Take a quick look around and you can see that's basically what we have done. We have effectively created a tollbooth economy: goods and money pass through and we take a slice, but the real long-term value accrues elsewhere. But the discovery of the NEO Economy had changed the entire game. When you are able to identify precisely those people who make their purchase decisions on a whole range of other factors in addition to price, you can start to unlock the opportunities for goods and services that reflect the higher costs of more personalized service, uniqueness and design.

Since many of the jobs created to meet this demand must not only be started here but must stay here, the economic impact of this can be profound. They are 'baked in to the cake'–you simply can't buy local produce from somewhere else, nor have a personal relationship with someone who has no real-world connection to you, no matter how clever the technology or low the price.

A dollar generated in a tollbooth economy is worth considerably less in terms of its overall economic impact (the multiplier effect), than one in a NEO Economy, where a higher proportion of the benefits remain here.

And this isn't about Nationalism, Protectionism, or any other 'ism' that has routinely failed throughout economic history. It's simply about recognizing what is valued by a vital part of our population and giving it to them.

Articulating these insights allowed us to see clearly the degree to which the unmet wants, desires and needs of NEOs – this powerful economic group – could provide the solution not just to any one business' success (though it could certainly do that) but could, in fact, form the basis of a New American Economy.

In many places, the highly individualized and powerful NEOs did have a wide choice of where they bought their food, which coffee shops they frequented or what type of technology they used, but when it came to the company with whom they banked, invested or insured with, or what type of healthcare they bought or what type of energy they consumed, where was the real choice? These providers were much of a much-ness.

For every Traditional business there was latent demand for at least one and possibly many NEO alternatives, but often little or no supply. Our excitement began to mount.

But we're getting way ahead of ourselves. Before we go on, we have to answer two questions: what are the denizens of each planet really like, and how is it that NEOs can wield such great economic clout yet apparently have remained undetected up until now?

CHAPTER THREE
WELCOME TO THE TWO PLANETS

Planet NEO

Despite representing just under one-quarter of the population, NEOs wield powerful social and economic clout. They are the ones buying the new technology and personal services—all those tablet computers, 4G phones, personal trainers, farmers' market breads and craft beers—and they also spend prolifically on travel, eating out, drinking, investing and an entire range of services that make their lives easier, more individual and more controllable.

According to our most recent round of research, completed in April 2012, NEOs are six times more likely than Traditionals to eat in a restaurant on a daily basis, and measurably more likely to spend more when they do.

They are twice as likely as Traditionals to attend further education; they fill our universities, take professional roles, and executive positions. Ultimately, they are shaping the society that we all live in, and their influence is growing as the economic power base shifts from Traditionals to this New Economic Order.

As well as the 59 million NEOs in America, there are six million in Canada, four million in Australia, and 12 million in the UK.

There is a direct line from the bustling scene at The Kitchen Café in Boulder, Colorado, where you can get outstanding meals sourced from local suppliers such as the nearby Long's Farm, to The Monmouth

Coffee Company off a back street in London's theatre district, where they will make you an individual cup from your choice of hand-roasted beans sourced from locally owned coffee plantations around the world, and then on to the handmade, individually designed shoes from Jodie Fox's Shoes of Prey in Sydney, Australia. Different countries, different price points, different business models, but each of them shares the NEO customer's thirst for authenticity, discovery, and individuality.

Although NEOs tend to be metropolitan dwellers, with more of them living in inner urban areas than anywhere else, there are NEOs in every state of the Union. Forty five percent of NEOs are women and 55 percent are men. Whilst NEOs range over all age groups, they tend to be younger than Traditionals. There are plenty of 70-year-old NEOs, just as there are lots of 20-year-old Traditionals (remember age is just a date of manufacture), however NEOs and Evolvers dominate every age category under 50. This means that in 10 years' time the NEO/Evolvers will dominate every area of business, making this an opportunity that continues to grow in the future. We are in the middle of a seismic shift affecting where the economic power lies in America and around the world. It couldn't have happened at a better time.

NEOs love the internet and live much of their lives online. In fact NEOs are a remarkable nine times more likely than Traditionals to be classified as Heavy Internet Users, whether this is through home and office or, increasingly, mobile devices. Online they can exert individual control and accelerate what we call slow time. They do this by taking care of banking, share trading, travel bookings, music and movie purchasing, and anything else that saves time and allows them to jettison mundane tasks. The web is a place where NEOs can indulge their desire to discover things for themselves and establish their own conclusions away from the world of mass media. Sites such as Yelp, with its independent reviews of local businesses, are NEO Nirvana.

NEOs also dominate all heavy media consumption; newspaper and magazine readership, arts participation, internet usage, subscription TV viewership, addressed mail readership and even participation in the arts. This creates a new consumer currency for marketers and publishers alike. We have seen that "males aged between X and Y" is irrelevant as a measure of spending propensity, so it makes little sense to continue to invest advertising dollars on this basis. Instead, being able to know which media appeal to high spending NEOs or deal-hungry Traditionals should be the main determinant when it comes to choosing marketing channels and the type of message and products offered. The efficiencies to be had in marketing spend alone should make most businesses sit up and take notice.

NEOs trust people and small businesses. They don't trust media (although they don't distrust it in the Palin-esque "Lame Street Media" manner), big business, governments, or politicians. They insist on individuality. When it comes to a NEO as consumer, they make their evaluations on the experience of consumption as a whole. In terms of customer service, they look for the personal solution, the tailored, the idiosyncratic, something that evolves over time and keeps them engaged. Telling a NEO 'your' policies (as in 'we can't do that, it's not our policy') is an affront to their sense of self. When they are engaged it is the *experience* that is far more important than the transaction for them, far more important than the deal. There is no such thing as too much information for a NEO. They like it rich, dense, and preferably narrowcast, and expect it to be available at their demand, 24/7.

They show a marked preference for the authentic, and gravitate towards products and services that can tell true, authentic stories of provenance and uniqueness. They follow 'the whispered secret' and love the process of discovery. They are not led by fads, won't be talked down to, targeted, or influenced by the mainstream or what is "popular." For NEOs, the edge is the only place to be. They understand and embrace change, and for them experience is inextricably entwined with design, which acts as code for the attention to detail that is a gateway to uniqueness. This does not mean that NEOs are 'anti-brands,' they are not, as they tend to view them as a shortcut to quality. But the types of brands that appeal to NEOs are those which fit the values that drive the NEO Economy.

If you are a NEO or Evolver, you are probably starting to realize that not only is your individualism potentially powerful, you aren't the only one who views the world this way. Those two things may seem contradictory (*a group of individuals?*) but understanding how that works is critical to understanding NEOs.

As soon as we start ascribing characteristics to NEOs, it's tempting to start making broad assumptions about the entire group. Nothing could be further from the point. It is their very individualism that defines a NEO, so the moment we start to become prescriptive (instead of descriptive) we are back in the mind-set of social segmentation and we will miss the point. This is the old, unhelpful approach that assigns incremental values to someone based upon some data such as birthdate (think Yuppies, Dinkies, Slackers, and Millennials) while ignoring the inconvenient facts that don't fit a particular social segmentation.

Having an iPhone doesn't make you a NEO; just as buying on price alone some of the time doesn't make you a Traditional. It is the set of factors (values and attitudes) that drive our behaviors, not always the observed behaviors themselves that is the key determinant here. One of the most NEO people we know, who runs a business 100 percent orientated to creating extraordinary experiences for his clients, has never owned a cell phone. Wouldn't dream of it. It is individuality that defines NEOs and defines the NEO economy.

Planet Traditional

Traditionals tend to hold conformist social attitudes, are reluctant spenders, and careful investors.

Over on Planet Traditional, whether the price is high (for status) or low, it is *always* a dominant factor. It is worth reiterating here that it's not that NEOs implicitly *want* to spend more than Traditionals. It's just that price, while always a factor, tends not to be the dominant one for them when it comes to products and services for which they have a high engagement factor. Where engagement is low, price becomes a more dominant factor. In fact, for NEOs, ticket price is often be the cost of falling in love, in that they have already personally connected with the product or service before they even consider the price.

Remember, that this has little to do with income or wealth levels. Ever price-sensitive, Traditionals are far more interested in features, functions and the right deal than they are in quality and a premium relationship. What is often perceived as their brand loyalty is actually loyalty to the overall deal—a particular combination of price, features and status. If a better deal comes along they will switch to whoever is offering it. When it comes to customer service, they may look as though they are more tolerant of being treated as part of a marketing category than NEOs are, but this is purely because they believe that they have little chance of influencing the transaction and, in general, they demonstrate a greater deference to authority. Make no mistake; they will switch brands, companies or suppliers as soon as a viable alternative with a better deal appears.

For business leaders whose customers are predominantly Traditionals or whose product has become commoditized, everything else becomes secondary to establishing the answer to "are we the number one deal in the eyes of our potential customers?" This is a harsh reality and often contrary to the career goals and personal aims of inhabitants of the C suite, but it is vital none the less.

What About the Economy?

One thing that interested us greatly was the impact on consumer spending of massive shocks to the economy, such as the onset of the Great Recession. We saw that Traditionals would spend big during periods of perceived economic safety, leading to widespread splurges of consumption during the good years (big houses, big cars and big toys). But they would be equally aggressive in tightening their belts when the future was uncertain. Given that there are 120 million Traditionals, these wild yet predictable swings cause the booms and busts of the trade cycle to be exacerbated. They only start to loosen the purse string a little once they start to feel "safe" to do so again. An economy rooted on the consumption spending of Traditionals can wait an awful long time for that to happen.

NEOs operated very differently. They tended to have a stronger view of their own personal economy and were generally far more optimistic about their prospects. This meant that although they were as freaked out as everyone else after the attacks of 9/11 and the market crash of 2008, they resumed their normal spending measurably sooner than Traditionals. This explained how, while the economy struggled greatly after the economic shock of 2008, spending did not meltdown in the manner that the media told the story, it fell but not by the levels the headlines would have predicted it did if everyone behaved in the same way. As NEOs are the predominant spenders in society, their economic resilience kept the wheels turning, even while Traditionals were heading for the spending bunkers.

It is vital to understand that this has very little to do with wealth. For both traditional economic theorists and social protestors, the emphasis is always on individual wealth—the assumption is that wealth is the key factor in spending decisions. But despite the demographic breakdowns or talk of 1% vs 99%, wealth has surprisingly little influence on spending. During downturns, wealthy Traditionals cut back on their spending—in relative terms—every bit as much as lower income Traditionals.

Traditionals did sometimes buck their bargain-seeking image. Many were willing to spend lavishly on special events, such as weddings, parties or vacations. In fact, despite their tendency towards economic conservatism, in these categories spending more than their peers on a bigger wedding, fancier party or even bigger blow-out in Vegas was almost a source of pride. But the key thing here was frequency—how often they acted like this. High spending happens occasionally among Traditionals, it just doesn't happen very frequently compared to NEOs. And when it does happen, it tends to be event-driven.

Engagement as the Deciding Factor

It can be confusing to consider the circumstances in which NEOs, Evolvers and Traditionals all behave the same way. But it's important to understand this point of intersection in order to set your personal course. Indeed, thinking through the way we've described the two groups may have left you feeling you have both NEO and Traditional characteristics. But once you start to look at the types of decisions you make, and consider which have a great deal of personal engagement and which that are purely functional, the picture becomes clearer.

A good example is a partner we know in a major actuarial firm, not the normal habitat of NEOs. When it comes to food, cars, housing and various other things he is every inch driven by the great deal. But it turns out that he really cares very little about these factors and so has low engagement with them. One car is very much the same to him, as is where he buys his groceries. But ask him about his passions and another picture emerges. He is an avid climber and when he buys his climbing gear, who he buys it from is every bit as important as what he buys. He will drive hundreds of miles to meet the guy who is building his rack, and wax lyrical for hours about one type of clamp over another. He feels the same about his technology and his whisky. When it comes to his areas of passion and engagement, all of the price considerations go out of the window. He may not be your typical NEO...but that is because there is no such thing as a typical NEO.

Think about toothpaste for a moment. When it comes to this basic purchase, the level of engagement for both NEO and Traditionals is pretty low. Most just buy the one that is the best deal, either because of brand preference (Colgate vs. Crest), promotion (a free toothbrush) or some feature such as tooth whitening or new added wonder chemical. Statistically there is very little distinction between the two planets. But even here there are exceptions.

Tom and Kate Chappell started Tom's of Maine in 1970 with just $5,000 and the idea that they could make toothpaste and other body-care products that were not chemically derived, tested on animals or harmful to the environment. They did this long before any of these were considered marketing features; they were simply working to meet their own ideals. As it happens, these ideals rate very highly for NEOs and Evolvers. By the time the Chappell's sold the company in 2006, it was worth $100 million, having established a very profitable, high-margin position in one of the most competitive markets segments, going head to head with some of the most sophisticated and biggest budgeted marketers in the world. This was the perfect encapsulation of the fact that in the NEO Economy it is passion that drives engagement. NEOs are defined by their individuality, which means that caring about the ethics of your toothpaste is far from universal even among NEOs. But those people who did care about these issues *and* were prepared to pay accordingly were predominantly NEOs. The Chappell's product provided them with a NEO option in a sea of mega brands and international competitors, and its creators were richly rewarded.

Does all of this mean that every business can only have either NEOs or Traditionals in its consumer base? Not at all. We've already seen that when it comes to commodities, both types of consumer appear to behave in the same way, and additionally each can have a very different relationship with a product.

Lexus cars provide a great example of something that both NEOs and Traditionals buy using utterly different strategies. Broadly speaking, it may be the design, technology or some other individual factor that draws the Neo to a Lexus showroom. He or she will arrive there having fully briefed themselves on all of the vehicles' features, read multiple reviews online and built their own version on the Lexus website. They have most likely come to do what they can't do online, which is to touch and test-drive the car, exploring the experience of it. That experience will be their deciding factor. They will also have researched the price, knowing everything from dealer cost to what other people have paid for the same product elsewhere in the state and country.

In contrast, Traditionals are likely to know a great deal less about the car's features and will require more detailed explanation. The price they are willing to pay plays a far more significant role in their decision. That means that if the BMW or Mercedes dealer down the road is offering a deal that day on something that has more features or perceived higher status, then a Traditional is much more likely to consider a BMW or Mercedes as an alternative to a Lexus. Their decision will be based on whichever car can hit the right mix of status, feature and deal.

Figuring out what's really going on in that transaction means being able to identify and understand the consumer behind it. What you never have in a Lexus showroom, or anywhere else, is "an average customer." Despite the fact that both NEOs and Traditionals buy cars and, indeed, NEOs buy cars more often than Traditionals, it is pretty clear who most of the marketing targets and nearly all of the car salespeople are trained to deal with.

Whenever we explain NEOs and Traditionals and the Two Planet principle, we get asked the same questions: Where were the NEOs before this, and why hasn't anyone noticed them up until now? We asked ourselves the very same thing. The research shows us that what makes someone a NEO or a Traditional is innate (so maybe there were Cro-Magnon NEOs scanning the horizon, waiting for a Paleolithic Steve Jobs to come along and bring them an Apple Mac carved from stone). We decided to flip the question on its head and ask, 'At what point did the environment afford NEOs the opportunities to come out in force?'

In answering this, we began to see the emergence of NEO economic power as the result of an unprecedented combination of factors which created a 'virtuous cycle' that is irrevocably changing the socio-economic landscape in its wake. And, yes, that does needs some explaining.

CHAPTER FOUR
THE EARTH SHIFTS BENEATH OUR FEET

Having recognized the two fundamentally distinct types of consumers, we found ourselves coming back again and again to the question of whether the existence of NEOs was a new development. Was it caused by some relatively recent human or economic factor, such as a deep and long lasting recession or the invention of the internet, or has there always been this distinction and we were just giving voice to it? If it was new, what caused it? If it had always been in place, why had it taken so long to be fully recognized?

Over the 10 years' worth of data we studied, the values and attitudes that drove NEOs and Traditionals proved highly consistent on an individual level. In other words, when it came to spending money on things with which they had a high engagement level, not one person moved from the highly individualistic and more wide ranging NEO drivers over to the much more predictable Planet Traditional drivers, or vice versa. Not one.

It was accepted wisdom that the difference in consumers' actions was tied to the difference in income levels, but as we now knew, when we considered *how* they actually went about spending it, income was not the key factor at all. A NEO faced with the aftermath of the global economic meltdown of 2008 continued to spend on things that reflected their own personal values (including uniqueness, design and authenticity), just as a Traditional continued to make their decisions almost exclusively on the basis of price, features and status, even if what they spent it on changed. If people's approach to consuming remained essentially consistent in even in the most threatening economic environment for almost 80 years, we had to consider the possibility that this was not a recent behavioral development, but was instead inherent. The only way to know for sure was to look back through history for clues.

Prior to the Industrial Revolution, the very concept of discretionary spending was limited to a tiny number of people. The vast majority of the population either lived the sort of much romanticized but materially deprived subsistence life of the homesteader or, a level below this, in the type of poverty that can be seen in much of the Third World today. When life hangs by a thread, dependent upon the next crop or the whims of those in power (aristocracy and landholders in 18th century Europe, warlords in modern day Somalia), people can't express much of themselves other than the thirst for survival.

In North America and Europe this started to change with the onset of industrialization in the early 19th century. Large numbers of people moved from the country to the rapidly expanding cities. Technological developments including proper plumbing and clean water followed, and some of the most time-consuming tasks got quicker and easier. Factories, roads, and railways revolutionized what was produced, how it was produced and where it could be distributed. The jobs that were created resulted in more people becoming specialists, able to perform a limited number of tasks. They then used the income they received to buy goods and services from others.

Initially, many workers were paid so little and worked so hard that they had essentially exchanged the poverty of the farm for the equal poverty of the city. But over time it became clear to the business owners of the day that if the workers were not paid enough and had no free time, there was not enough of a market for their products. It wasn't just the increasing organization of labor or any particular goodwill of an entrepreneurial class that led to increases in the standard of living of 19th Century workers, but the self-interest of the companies who needed customers too.

Without setting out to do so, this laid the foundations of our consumer economy, developing a "mass market" that simply hadn't existed before. There might not yet have been any bumper stickers or talk shows decrying the "outsourcing" of jobs that moved from the country to the cities, but that's what was happening. Increasing numbers of people were feeding themselves and their families by working the machines that produced the goods they now needed to buy. The competition for skilled labor had begun and so had the emergence of new industries, such as the manufacture of clothing, which had previously been primarily done within the home. The wheels of capitalism began to turn and what we would recognize as the modern consumer economy emerged.

From today's perspective, the past can look like a linear pathway: a series of logical steps leading to our present. But it's rarely, if ever, like that, and the development of the consumer economy certainly wasn't. It relied on an accumulation of seemingly unrelated developments, things that at the time appeared to be abrupt and sometimes radical changes, which can only be connected with the benefit of hindsight.

For example, two instances of these unrelated changes crucial to the development of a consumer economy were the harnessing of electricity and the relaxing of puritan attitudes that were replaced by an ethos of individualism. In 1910 domestic electricity was available in only 10 percent of American homes but by 1917 it had been extended to a market for domestic electrical appliances of $175 million annually ($3.3 billion in 2011 money)—a remarkable figure, given that the population was just 103 million. Meanwhile, social standards and views were changing. American society had moved from puritanism and what historian William Leach calls "early traditions of republicanism and Christian virtue" to an increasingly forward-looking culture of individualism. On its launch in 1948, Estée Lauder's cosmetic company rapidly became a huge success. But had she started the company just four or five decades earlier, amidst any lingering Puritanical dictates that forbade women to wear makeup or enhance their appearance in any way, things would have been very different. The face creams that went down a storm when she opened her first store in on 5th Avenue would have been met with a very different response.

Kellogg's, Coca-Cola, Procter & Gamble, Kodak, and Ford are all examples of companies that set their sights on this new mass market and established a business model for success. They launched, produced products at price points that were within reach of as many consumers as possible, and then built brands through advertising in print and the new channel of radio. In this way, they each established recognition and ultimately category dominance. It was a formula for success that allowed them to even survive the Depression, which killed off many of their competitors, searing that business model into the psyche of what was to become Corporate America.

Following the Depression and World War II there was both a new spirit of unfettered consumerism and a growing number of people with the money to indulge in what American economist Thorstein Veblen first labeled 'conspicuous consumption'. Certain kinds of clothing, cars, homes, furniture and jewelry became symbols of the new wealth; the notion of a particular aspirational 'lifestyle' was created, packaged and sold. Think of the rise from poverty of Don Draper in the AMC show *Mad Men*, with the seemingly perfect wife and children at home and the opportunity to build his career on his own talents, free from the social constraints of past generations. That is how the story was supposed to go, anyway.

The mass market was gaining force, as was the concept of a widely accessible American Dream complete with a white picket-fenced house in the suburbs, membership of a country club and working one's way up the corporate ladder. Looking at these values now it is easy to see them as typical of Planet Traditional. But not everyone fit the mold. The 1961 Richard Yates novel *Revolutionary Road* (turned into an Oscar-nominated 2008 film) is a cautionary tale about people we would now call NEOs trying to squeeze themselves into a Traditional slot. Frank and April Wheeler meet in the New York of the late 1940s and, young and optimistic, plan to move to Paris and experience freedom. Instead they move to a suburban home and try their best to conform. It doesn't go well. With no way to live out their individual NEO dreams and desires, the Wheelers find themselves straitjacketed by Traditional expectations.

Yates' book is fiction, not documentary, but it accurately reflects the reality that there have always been people who seemingly had it all, yet didn't fit the narrative of wider society. The industrial revolution laid the groundwork for the emergence of consumer mass market in the mid-20th century by emphasizing and rewarding conformity. (Conformity in some sense is still very attractive to many people today, whether it's a desire to return to the heyday of the unions on the political left, or the reinstallation of strict version 'family values' from those on the right.)

This conformity leaves no place for NEOs to be seen. They are either excluded from our understanding of society as outliers or, much more feasibly, simply become invisible. With no way to express their individuality, they appear to be part of the Traditional mass market. They are, in effect, hiding in plain sight and the economic power they have remains unharnessed

The answer to the question 'Where have the NEOs been up until now,' is 'Right in front of us, but dormant in the circumstances.' Prior to the Industrial Revolution, NEOs were economically invisible, toiling shoulder to shoulder with those we would now call Traditionals, all barely subsisting. Later they were employed in the factories that fuelled the industrial revolution, again without opportunity to express their innate NEO desires. Against the conformity of much of the American society of the 1950s, '60s and '70s they were forced to the edges. Only recently, and only in certain parts of the world, have the various necessary developments come together, allowing NEOs to emerge to center stage, as a force in their own right.

So, NEOs as an active force are relatively new, but they're not brand new. Why did no one notice them before us? Well, on occasion they did see all the evidence—there have long been observations of the type of behavior that we can now categorize as representing NEOs. But seeing and understanding are two different things. Those who have observed what we now recognize as defining NEO behavior have always viewed it, and skewed it, through existing filters of consumer behavior.

Even when the evidence has been before them, NEO behavior has been attributed to factors such as income, demographic, or education, or what they do has been labeled as a 'social trend'. Only by using rigorous science and huge quantities of data was the truth revealed: to understand our consumer economy and who is driving it today we needed to drop all those existing filters and really see what had been in front of us all along.

We "discovered" NEOs because our curiosity had been piqued: we needed to be able to explain to ourselves the anomalies and contradictions in their patterns of consumption and so we embarked on the research that revealed their distinct presence, traits and characteristics. Simply put, no one before us noticed NEOs in quite the way we had because no-one else asked questions we did.

Why didn't they? To answer that, think about why all classical Venetian paintings seem to be of noblemen and religious figures. Because that's who paid the bill for the paintings to be done. The market research that was done over decades to establish all the accepted wisdom about who buys what, and when and why they do it, was being done from the perspective of Traditionals, the mass market, and finding niches within that. It could not identify what it wasn't designed to look for.

The research unconsciously reflected the expectations of those who were footing the bill. Many of the consumer businesses that became huge successes during the period of the economic dominance of Traditionals emphasized the brand, the product's features and, where relevant, the price (either high or low). This became the unquestioned model for how businesses should be built. The whole raft of support services that emerged to take care of these businesses--advertising, marketing and public relations--developed a way of talking about consumers that was based on this way of doing business.

Any desire to explore new ways of doing things, to develop products and services and often business models, was lost amid the practice of benchmarking what had been done before and mimicking the elements of past successes. It is hard to drive far forward when you are navigating through the rear view mirror. With Traditionals in control, the way forward was always likely to be based upon what had happened in the past, even if the evidence of change was right in front of their noses.

It may also be that another reason no one asked the question is because of how we experience change itself. In England, historians suggest that the Industrial Revolution began around the second half of 1700s, yet the first use of the term 'industrial revolution' doesn't seem to have happened until 1827, sixty years after the invention of the spinning jenny and 58 years after the invention of the steam engine. Much later again, in 1884, economic historian Arnold Toynbee gave the first series of lectures on the industrial revolution, explaining the term and outlining the social and economic effects. Only then did the idea that there had been an industrial revolution really take hold. Historical shifts only become recognizable movements in hindsight.

So, it makes sense that it was only with the value of hindsight that we could see the pattern of seemingly unrelated events that together created a juddering shift in the economic landscape surrounding us. As anyone who has ever lost a job, got divorced, or had a major life event will testify, it's difficult to really understand change when you're in the middle of it.

Another Revolution

This led us to another huge question—whose answer might have extraordinary implications. If modern consumer society as we recognize it today emerged as a result of the convergence of numerous specific factors following the Industrial Revolution was there perhaps a whole new set of factors that had emerged and converged, creating the momentum that allowed consumers to polarize into NEOs and Traditionals? If so, could it be that the economic downturn that began in 2007 is simply accelerating and bringing in to sharper focus the shifts that were already irrevocably altering the landscape? Was the Great Recession brutally exposing changes that were already happening, rather than being the agent of change itself?

With this in mind we started to look at the societal changes, particularly those that gained strength in the 1960s, which embraced the spirit of individualism and self expression that are key defining traits of NEOs. After the relatively constrained world of the post-war period, America became a more nuanced place. There began to be room for the more individualistic members of society to express who they were. The Cuban Missile Crisis, the civil rights movement, the Vietnam War, and the social and sexual liberation of the hippie era fundamentally changed the social landscape, as did Watergate in the 1970s. The narrative of the country shifted from white-bread simplicity of *Leave it to Beaver* to the subversive, sarcastic, iconoclastic *All in the Family*, right through to the convention-busting satire of *Modern Family*.

But society becoming more accepting of what would previously have been seen as unacceptably non-conformist behavior wasn't the only factor. Other key elements converged to facilitate the emergence and economic accession of the New Economic Order.

The Drive Towards Commoditization

Ironically, the success of a model marked by keystones of commodity, conformity and ubiquity, increasingly created something for those who didn't share those values to align themselves against. When all food came from farms nearby, restaurants were owned by people who lived in the same town and every neighborhood had a distinct character, there wasn't much for the individualistic Neo to react against. Fast forward to a time when, other than the weather, it's hard to tell suburban Seattle from suburban Atlanta and every "neighborhood" has an Applebee's, Staples, and Starbucks. With so many businesses run by distant corporations, the rebellious NEO is spoilt for choice in what to dislike, even if they are not always sure why. Conformity actually creates the circumstances for differentiation.

Capitalism craves commoditization. It is, as we have seen, simply the most 'efficient' way to operate and grow a large business. It's often said that globalization has made the world more commoditized, more homogenized. When the product or service is essentially the same, each town or country is in competition with all others and capital is directed towards those that offer the best deal (lower prices, incentives, available skilled labor, etc.). But it may be that, in fact, the reverse is true: commoditization is driving globalization.

Given that Planet Traditional is driven primarily by price, features and status, something that is valued only according to these factors can be produced almost anywhere. So it was only a matter of time before business owners pushed past geographic boundaries to reach countries that could offer the same means of production at even lower prices. Leveraging economies of scale in a global marketplace makes it possible to offer better deals on things that previously might have been available only at extravagant prices, such as big screen TVs, which appeal to both Traditionals and NEOs as, essentially, a commodity, differentiated only by price, brand (status) and the number of features (HDMI ports, picture-in-picture facility, etc).

There are plenty of examples of this strategy bringing huge success. Walmart provides the playbook, with operations that are gargantuan in scale. According to its 2010 company report, Wal-Mart has more than 200 million 'customer and member' transactions each week. It has "more than 8,576 retail units" in 15 countries; its 2010 sales revenue was $405 billion; and it employs "more than 2.1 million associates" worldwide. This success story is directly related to Walmart sticking close to the values that drive its customer base--the best deals on products that are going to appeal to both Traditionals and NEOs, with price, features, and status the only distinguishing factors.

Exxon Mobil, CVS Caremark, Kroger, Costco, and a host of other companies have been able to execute essentially the same strategy with massive success. They are using the cost cutting power of commoditization, and its stepchild globalization, to their advantage. They deliver exactly what almost all consumers want when they are buying commoditized products, which works to their own advantage, and to the advantage of their customers, too. Nobody "wants" to pay more for any of the products they sell, so finding the lowest possible cost base is essential.

However, when we start to look at the quality rather than just quantity of jobs that are created by this economic shift, the picture is much less rosy. Increasingly we are seeing massive reductions in the middle-class jobs that provided the economic vibrancy and growth of previous decades. In their place has come more low-skilled, low-benefit, low-paid jobs. Again, this is not a criticism of these companies. When your business is founded upon the 'great deal,' it is essential that you use all the tools at your disposal in order to provide this deal before someone else does.

But the success of large companies in creating a world where every Target store has the same colors, fixtures and products as every other Target store, in every other city or even country, laid the groundwork for a counter-movement from those who are in search of premium relationships, unique products with a sense of provenance, and the authenticity of dealing with people who are passionate about their product, not just employees of a major company working for a pay-check. Commoditization and the homogenization it brings with it galvanizes NEOs, pushing them into a fierce rejection of these values in pursuit of the unique and authentic.

How Do You Like Your Eggs?

If you want to see how NEOs act when faced with the march of commoditization, just take a quick trot through the last forty years of meat, dairy and poultry sales. Such a snapshot serves as a perfect example of how homogenization can create great deals while triggering an entirely new marketplace to meet NEO demands.

It's an oddity that in our lifetimes we have gone full circle from eggs coming from chickens that spent their time wandering around a farmyard, through battery hens being the norm, and back to free-range eggs, only this time as an option for which some consumers (primarily NEOs and Evolvers) willingly pay a premium. Go back far enough and the term 'free-range' didn't exist; it didn't need to, because there wasn't any alternative to differentiate. In fact, there was little to differentiate any of the meat, poultry or cheese that you could buy. It all just came from the farm.

The onset of factory farming and the introduction of the supermarket turned meat, poultry and cheese into commodities that could be mass produced and sold at what previous generations would have considered unbelievably low prices. But in order to drive prices down so far, the 'factory' part of factory farming resulted in livestock being kept in what some consumers consider inhumane conditions, and also in meat they consider to be of inferior quality. (The old line "it tastes like chicken" only works because mass produced chicken doesn't really taste of anything other than what you put on it.)

The events that unfolded when a UK supermarket introduced a £2 chicken are a perfect demonstration of the increasingly polarized world-views of NEOs and Traditionals. In 2006, the supermarket chain Asda (owned by Walmart) put whole cooked chickens on sale at the unprecedentedly low price of just £2 each (about $3). This particular promotion was leapt on by celebrity TV chef Jamie Oliver, who launched a campaign to draw public attention to the conditions in which these chickens had been kept. His anti-battery hen campaign was supported by other public figures, including fellow celebrity foodie Hugh Fearnley-Whittingstall. Asda's publicity department was soon struggling to deal with the negative press and direct feedback it was getting from irate soon-to-be-ex customers, with plenty of media coverage.

There is another side to this story, though. The chickens were selling like crazy. Cynics and most social commentators dismissed this fact by saying it just showed that no matter what consumers might say, at the checkout they lacked the courage of their convictions. By now, though, you will have realized that the apparent contradiction between the outcry and the sales figures is nothing of the sort. The residents of Planet NEO were protesting vigorously against what they saw as another undesirable step towards a homogenized world.

Simultaneously, but completely separately, the citizens of Planet Traditional were enthusiastically saying, "Mmmm, chicken tonight!"

For NEOs, turning away from mass market supermarkets in favor of specialist, local producers is not just a matter of animal welfare or reducing food miles (although for many those things matter). It's also about the quality of the produce they are purchasing and the authenticity of the buying experience. Many NEOs love seeking out the specialist stores where they can learn the name of the farm from which their produce comes, or request a single slice of Stinking Bishop cheese, cut to order and wrapped in wax paper. The enjoyment they get from eating the cheese or meat hours or days later is enhanced by the experience they had when they bought it. Many NEOs won't think twice about paying a premium for grass-fed beef, wild salmon, or free-range lamb, whereas most Traditionals see all this as a marketing gimmick aimed at suckers. To them, meat is meat.

Commoditization alone would be enough to create the twin polarities of the Traditionals' search for the extraordinary deal and the NEOs' quest for the extraordinary further, but something else has pushed this process to a whole new level. Advances in technology, specifically the availability of the worldwide web as a tool, have both flattened the global market and allowed even finer consumer distinctions and definitions to be drawn.

The Internet—Simultaneously Flattening and Opening Up the World

Thirty years ago, most of us relied upon mainstream media as the primary source of our information, and local retailers sold us most of what we bought. The diffusion of new communication technology and the advent of social media and search engines changed all that.

Again, our research shows that NEOs are nine times more likely than Traditionals to be heavy web users. NEOs love new technology and love the web because it allows them to both explore new experiences and gain more control--they can accelerate slow time, move things off of their plates and free up time for more of what they *want* to do, not have to do. Even though information-hungry NEOs are voracious consumers of magazines and books (they are four times more likely to read books than anyone else), the internet provides a faster, more flexible, more relevant source of information that they readily use to dig deeper into whatever products, services or suppliers capture their interest and to search for deals when they are buying something that's been commoditized.

Social media sites and their precursors, chat rooms, have created an environment where like-minded people can share information in a way that was simply not possible 30, 20, or even ten years ago. NEOs don't trust the mass media, nor do they trust big businesses, but they do trust their peers. They hate being targeted as part of a large group or market segment. They prefer to find out information about products or services for themselves, and will go online to share opinions and experiences with people like them.

The net creates communities formed around interests, which means that NEOs can coalesce around ideas and concepts, which in turn creates a polarizing effect upon attitudes and behaviors. The same factors are at play on Planet Traditional, but in a different way. For each group, there is an ever-increasing polarization of experience, perception and, ultimately, ideology. Quite literally, we no longer have to listen to anyone who doesn't already agree with us.

The internet also creates a larger market for unique and individual products because you're not just tied down to what you can buy in person near you. To go back to the NEO rejection of commoditized, homogenized food in favor of the extraordinary or the unique, even those NEOs who can't visit their favored specialist butcher, fishmonger, or cheese-maker can go on line and take a virtual journey through the back story of its fish, meat, and cheese, then purchase the product through the web site.

The first step in this journey might be sheer curiosity, but it will also reveal whether product is as authentic as it claims, or if any promise of authenticity it's just a construct of a marketing agency. Visit the website of any of the growing number of artisan cheese makers, such as Sonoma's Bellwether Farm (www.bellwtherfarms.com) or New York's Nettle Meadow Farm (www.nettlemeadow.com) and you'll see photographs not just of the people who make the cheese, but the places in which it is made and even the animals from which the milk comes.

Classic semiotic analysis might suggest that sites like this work because urban-dwelling NEOs are being invited to 'buy a slice of country life' in the cheese they order. In other words, it doesn't matter if you use a stock photo-library shot, as long as the grass is green, the hills rolling and the sky blue. But that completely misses the NEOs' attraction to authenticity. The web is the tool allowing NEOs to gather information on whatever it is they are buying, and to make judgments accordingly. Daisy the goat is a crucial player in the means of production and when the NEO is able to see how she lives, it provides greater reassurance of the quality of the cheese she helps create. She's not just a generic part of rural atmosphere; she is a fundamental element in the story that underpins the authenticity of the cheese.

The dissemination of new technology and the internet means that these days, if they wish to, customers may know almost as much about the marketplace as companies do themselves. A simple web search can provide you with information on how many Audi A4s were sold last month in a given part of the country, what was the dealer invoice price, what sort of incentives the company offered to dealers and the range of prices that customers paid. Not that many years ago nobody other than the owner of the auto dealer themselves had this information.

Information is power. Today's consumers have the means to search for people they want to deal with and exclude those who aren't the right fit, and it is the NEOs and Evolvers who are taking advantage of this. For companies that want NEOs in their customer base, transparency is essential; the web means that any material incongruence between who you say you are and who you really are can easily be revealed.

Even companies that generally get it right for NEOs have learned this, to their peril. Yoga-wear phenom Lululemon found this out in 2007, when it had to admit that its Vita Sea cotton weave garments did not contain seven percent seaweed, as claimed—in fact they didn't contain any seaweed. It was old media that broke the story, *The New York Times* commissioned a lab test and published the results, but new media, on the web, ensured that it became a very big deal. The problem seemed to originate with a supplier, unbeknownst to the company, but as Lululemon found, it's not possible to ignore even a genuine mistake when it affects your authenticity.

Commoditization and the ubiquity of information have done a great deal to change the playing field, and both Traditionals and NEOs can now express their values more acutely through their consumption than at any time in history. The Two Planets are spinning further apart and the void between them is growing wider. No matter how clever entrepreneurs, politicians, labor leaders, and CEOs are, none of them can create meaningful economic and social success without understanding this reality. Economic growth based upon the Traditional model requires the lowest costs, more features, and ever-stronger brands. This is the unfortunate reality of a globalized and commoditized world. The Traditional model is not broken; in fact in many ways it has never been healthier, which is one of the real reasons corporate profits are continuing to grow. But while it will remain the backbone of many elements of our economy, if we are to grow and flourish in the years ahead we are going to need something else as well.

Wish You Were There

To help us understand how we can go about building this "something else," we need to see how manifestly different the residents of Planet NEO and Planet Traditional are operating already, and how the web is allowing them to become even more distinct with each and every passing day. While the web is used much more heavily and perhaps more adroitly, by NEOs, both NEOs and Traditionals both bend it to their own needs. Clearly any business worth its salt needs a website, but it also needs to understand its consumers in order to know what that website should provide. How each of the two types goes about booking a vacation encapsulates this.

NEOs often use the net to search the globe for amazing, unique experiences--that adventure camping lodge on Vancouver Island where you can paddle a canoe around humpback and minke whales and have a salmon barbecue on the beach before falling asleep in a luxury tent with a king size four-poster bed, or the great little hotel in SoHo with the eclectic interiors and amazing patisserie next door. They will utilize all of the valued tools at their disposal, such as Trip Advisor and Yelp, to learn the experiences, good and bad, of other people who have stayed there. This acts as an individualistic and authentic counterpoint to the marketing on the typical hotel or resort website, where everything is always perfect, everyone is beautiful and "your business is important to them"—but not always important enough to answer your call or email straight away.

Often it is only after they have decided upon the destination that NEOs will start to think seriously about the price. But when they turn their attention to the deal, they do it with full focus. Sites such as kayak.com open multiple booking engines at once, so that often the hotel is competing against itself to offer the best deal. Don't kid yourself: if you have something listed for one price on one website and another elsewhere, they will find it.

One of our NEO clients was recently on a business trip to London. He wanted to stay at the stylish Hempel Hotel in West London, an expression of stunning modern design behind the classic facade of a row of townhouses. Visiting the hotel's website he found the rate of $800 a night, which he was more than able to pay. But opening up another site, lastminute.com, he saw a deal on an "unidentified 5-star hotel" within one mile of the city's Paddington railway station. Two clicks later, using Google Maps, he could confirm that the only 5-star hotel in that area was, in fact, The Hempel. He booked the hotel immediately and paid $300 per night for precisely the same type of room.

There is nowhere to hide in the NEO Economy.

By contrast, Traditionals use the web primarily to search for extraordinary deals. They can go online and search for something they recognize (safety is important to Traditionals when it comes to experience), so brand names play a major role. Their buying decision will, as ever, come down to the same three characteristics: price, status (brand) and features (free internet, late check outs, a breakfast bonus).

But even as the NEOs are searching the web for their ultimate experience and Traditionals are using it for virtual bargain hunting, with very few exceptions both will look online for the lowest possible air ticket to get them where they're going. Why? Because airlines have, almost entirely become commodities separated only by price, quirky staff, air mile loyalty programs, or baggage fees. Only Richard Branson's Virgin airlines offer any hope of anything truly distinct, but unfortunately it isn't an option in many markets (yet).

So, globalization has created a chasm between the extraordinary deal and the extraordinary, and the internet has simultaneously flattened the global marketplace and allowed consumer distinctions to be drawn. Does this give us all the information we need to create a sustainable model of economic growth, rebuild the American economy and drive long term job growth? Not quite.

Demographics Are Useful Sometimes, After All

As much as we decry demographics as indicators of propensity to spend, they do serve as a useful quantitative measure of distinct groups within a population. The data reveals that both NEOs and Traditionals are found across all age groups, but that NEOs (and Evolvers) dominate every adult age group under the age of 50. There are plenty of 70-year-old NEOs and 20-year-old Traditionals, but the weight of numbers is changing, meaning that the economic relevance of NEOs is only going to increase with time. For the countries, companies and individuals who learn how to harness the power of the New Economic Order, it can become a source of sustainable, renewable and high value economic growth for generations to come. Twenty or thirty years ago, the majority of NEOs were still in high school, trying to stretch their allowances or money from part-time menial jobs to cover the purchases they wanted to make. This meant that there were a lot more Evolving NEOs than today. Their values were the same but the resources weren't yet there.

Fast forward to today. The NEOs have graduated, built their careers and, increasingly, their own businesses; they are twice as likely as Traditionals to start a new venture. Having more disposable income lets them express their NEO-ness on an ever more consistent basis, where those options exist. They dominate every income category above $60,000 annually, and are five times more likely than Traditionals to earn in excess of $100,000. Remember, it is their internal values and drivers that make them NEOs, not their income level. The world is increasingly rewarding the individualistic, idea-adopting and technology-absorbing skills that many NEOs display. Simultaneously, the more conservative, authority-respecting outlook of Traditionals, who typically like to follow the rules, is increasingly becoming commoditized and rewarded less and less as competition from technology and elsewhere gets stronger every year.

This shows that the idea that consumer behavior is in a constant state of flux is all wrong. It's not a change "in" people and their circumstances that has created the dividing lines in our society, it's a change "of" people—a changing of the guard. Now that NEOs are out in force, so are opportunities within the Neo Economy. While "the 1%" may be getting all of the headlines, it is actually the 46 percent or 113 million Americans, who can be the great economic force we can rebuild the country upon. NEOs dominate the Big

Spender categories, not because they are buying the super high-priced and high status goods, but because of the sheer weight of their accumulated spending.

As we've already noted, they buy more, buy more consistently, and have the means and the desire to pay for a premium for unique products, services, and experiences. The lowest cost is not the be all and end all for them, so they don't have to rip up our entire society to win.

Once we had analyzed the demographic breakdown of those people we had already identified as NEOs, it became clear that the connection between all of the factors that allowed their emergence was every bit as strong as the chain of events that had created the mass market almost a century before. Each event had to occur in order for the next one to happen or for it to have economic relevance.

The success of commoditizing so many elements of our lives created the perfect thing for the rising tide of NEO individualism to push back against. Similarly the growth of technology made it possible for those people who value the unique and individual to be able to find what they are looking for. It also enabled them to cut through the onslaught of mass marketing to find one another. Add in the surge of demographic changes (NEOs getting older) and a global marketplace that is commoditizing almost everything while rewarding adaptation to new ways of working, living and communicating, and the perfect NEO storm has been created: a dynamic, self-perpetuating force that can revitalize our economy. We named this "The Virtuous Cycle."

While the industrial revolution created modern consumer society, the rolling phases of the Virtuous Cycle were generating something radically different: the consumer equivalents of whole new planetary systems: The Two Planets, one for NEOs and one for Traditionals and a vacuum for any economy, country, or individual caught in between.

Perhaps the way the Virtuous Cycle works is best illustrated by looking with fresh eyes at the history of Apple. The story of this extraordinary enterprise has been told many (too many, perhaps) times before, but never in quite the way we see it. By understanding the Virtuous Cycle it becomes clear why Apple's early years were such a white-knuckle ride, why Steve Job's return was to be so triumphant...and where the company should go from here without him.

CHAPTER FIVE
IT'S NOT "THE ECONOMY, STUPID"

Firebrand political consultant James Carville famously stuck the phrase "It's the economy, stupid" above the door of Bill Clinton's campaign strategy room in the run-up to the 1992 Presidential election. It was his way of keeping the team's focus on the parlous state of the economy when they went out to meet the press. So while the reporters were desperate to build up a story about whichever of the then candidate's peccadilloes was the day's gossip, Governor Clinton was waxing lyrical about how we could create prosperity and opportunity in America by building "an information superhighway." At the time, perhaps only Al Gore really knew what he was talking about, but it sure sounded better than Papa Bush's 'more of the same' or Ross Perot's forecasts of doom.

As we all know, this period heralded the Tech Boom, with a subsequent bust and then long-term changes in our economy. But the forces at play in the Virtuous Cycle—commoditization, globalization, rapid technological innovation and the sheer weight of numbers of demographics—were already at play. Once you understand how these factors interacted, and their subsequent impact upon the world around us, you look at history with a new eye.

Today everyone wants to be Apple. Shipping millions of iPads, iPhones, MacBooks, and iMacs each year, it seems to be deliver results that suggest that it exists in a parallel universe, untouched by the economic realities that batter everyone else. Perhaps more than any other company on the planet, Apple seems to intuitively understand what customer's want, even before they know for sure themselves. And even in the worst part of the recession, while virtually every other store in every mall across America was offering 50 percent to 80 percent discounts as a way to get 'frightened consumers' to spend, Apple Stores were packed with people ready to pay the full retail price then walk out with a big smile on their face.

It's easy to forget it wasn't always like this. In the warm glow of the eulogies for Steve Jobs and low-level hum of investors stressing about how replacement CEO Tim Cook will perform, it's easy to forget that there was a time when the company's decision-makers couldn't get rid of Jobs fast enough. If the Apple story is really a tale of Steve Jobs' genius, as it is often told, then how do we account for this epic fail? Genius by definition is inherent, it isn't taught. (If it were, the fees for an MBA in Genius would be outrageous.) Steve Jobs was indeed a genius, but maybe genius alone isn't nearly enough to achieve success if other crucial elements aren't in alignment? The more we came to understand about NEOs, the more we realized that the well-worn version of Apple's rise is missing some crucial parts, because it is told with little attention to perhaps the most important actors in the whole story, the ones who buy the product.

Apple launched in 1976 and from the very first, it aligned itself with NEOs and their desire to always be at the cutting edge of design and experience. After its initial success, it spent its second decade skirting the precipice of failure. That seems illogical until you remember the way the Virtuous Cycle works: NEOs need disposable cash in order to consume in a NEO way, but the products they are consuming need to match their values, too. In the beginning, there were gaps on both sides of the equation.

Back in the mid-to-late 1970s, most of the NEOs who wield so much economic clout today were without the funds to indulge their taste. Those who were already in the workplace were often stymied in their take-up of Apple products because the control of company spending was still firmly in the hands of Traditionals. So while Apple products did find an appreciative market in creative (and NEO-heavy) areas including graphic design and advertising, when those departments suggested other areas of their company might want to switch to Apple, they were generally met with blank incomprehension.

Equally important, the technology hadn't yet developed to the point where NEOs outside design and advertising could seize upon it. As someone who became an Apple Mac devotee, *The Hitchhiker's Guide to the Galaxy* author Douglas Adams, wrote in 1999, "I remember the first time I ever saw a personal computer [a Commodore PET]... it was quite a large pyramid shape, with a screen at the top about the size of a chocolate bar. I prowled around it for a while, fascinated. But it was no good. I couldn't for the life of me see any way in which a computer could be of any use in the life or work of a writer." As he continues, he initially thought of personal computers "as a kind of elaborate adding machine," and that's how they were developed, at first.

That changed fairly quickly, but what took much longer for Apple to achieve was affordability. Even if you were able to see or use for one of these new machines, they were very expensive. (Don't forget, that's not a barrier for NEOs as such, but they have to be able to see value, according to their internal criteria.) When Apple started out, the push to commoditization, and in turn globalization, was still in its early stages. Meaning the company had a long way to go before it could create anything within the financial reach of large numbers of NEOs, let alone Evolvers. Although the original product, the 1976 Apple I cost only $666, it was designed to be put together by an enthusiast, who would buy the basic circuit board, then add a keyboard and displays. By 1980 when the company created the user-friendly Apple III to compete with IBM's upcoming PC, it cost between $4,300 and $7,800, depending on the configuration. In 1988 an Apple Mac cost upwards of $5,000, way beyond the cost of a PC at the time.

So, it was a product people didn't yet think they needed, at a price most couldn't afford. But there was one more major barrier: there was no worldwide web. The internet was still a complex, specialist network used by engineers and scientists. (It wasn't until 1990 that Tim Berners-Lee created the worldwide web; even then, it took another four or five years before it started developing into what we know today.) That left only mainstream media for Apple to use in an attempt to build a customer base, forcing it in to the constructs of 30-second TV spots and full-page print ads. Although Apple approached these with its customary innovation and boldness, there is only so much information that you can get across this way.

(Contrast TV and print advertising to the later web videos of the designers and architects of the products waxing lyrical about how they defined a problem and then set about solving it, playing firmly into the NEOs' love of rich authentic information. Apple has always been great at advertising, but the web has enabled the company to reveal its soul to its prospective customers. The ever-expanding boundaries of technology also allowed Apple to turn its products in to experiences, for instance through iTunes and AppStore. This allowed users to create their own individual product, unlike any other in the whole world. Individualization is nectar to NEOs.)

Only the self-perpetuating momentum of the Virtuous Cycle, with all its vital elements (leaps in technology; globalization-led price drops; and direct-to-NEOs communication through the web), could have turned Apple into the commercial superstar it is today. Without these crucial pieces in place, Apple still would have had many things going for it: a brilliant visionary at the helm, committed hard-working employees in a rapidly expanding sector, and innovation at almost every level of the company; all of the things that many commentators prescribe as the building blocks for new companies and the American economy in the years ahead. But without the emergence of the customers prepared to pay for these things, Apple may well have been just another footnote in technology history.

As it is, Apple is a huge success, but if we are to benefit from the most important lessons in its meteoric rise, we need to understand how the company has harnessed the power of the Virtuous Cycle and the emergence of NEOs and Evolvers. Only by doing this can we lay the groundwork for an American economic renaissance based on the way the world is, not the way it used to be.

So let's go back and look more closely at a few critical junctures in Apple's history to see in detail how the Virtuous Cycle worked.

You can't talk about Apple's early days without mentioning Microsoft, begun by Bill Gates in 1975, a year before Steve Jobs founded Apple with Steve 'Woz' Wozniak. The computer industry was still taking its first tentative steps. The earliest computers weren't easy to use and couldn't do much beyond serving as those glorified calculators. Both Gates and Jobs believed in their potential to be something far more, but they took totally different approaches to making it happen. Gates worked methodically on the evolution of his early programs and business model, while Jobs, with Wozniak at his side, was intent on revolution.

This revolutionary stance extended to the culture of the company that began to grow beneath them, as Wozniak moved more to the engineering side and Jobs slotted into position as charismatic leader. Apple was one of the first companies to abandon traditional work practices in favor of an atmosphere more college-campus than highly corporate. Steve Jobs was a NEO and he created a company in his image.

Having created that first computer, the Apple 1, a machine that only computer hobbyists understood, they quickly moved on to the Apple II, launched in 1977. This was more attractive, easier to use and, crucially, thanks to Wozniak's developments, it had added features allowing it to display higher resolution graphics. Every subsequent edition of the early Apples added more functions and features, but it was the Mackintosh that was to finally draw a line in the new industry's sand.

Announced in what has become an iconic Orwellian *1984*-themed ad directed by Ridley Scott and shown during the Superbowl of the same year, it established a David and Goliath relationship between Apple and Microsoft, implying there was now a sexy, free-thinking, full-blooded alternative to the corporate coldness and uniformity of Microsoft. It is little-known fact that the ad was conceived two years earlier, for the Apple II, but the board of the company hated it so much that they nearly fired the advertising firm Chiat/Day. Only the staunch support of Jobs and an offer by Steve Wozniak to personally pay for the air-time persuaded them to run what was to become one of the most famous adverts of all time. The Macintosh, and with it Apple, were launched in to the national consciousness.

The Macintosh's design backed up the implied promise of individuality in a grey corporate world. It might look clunky to us now, but at the time, in contrast to the PCs of the day, it looked gorgeous, and its point-and-click mouse was truly revolutionary. This was the moment Jobs truly defined Apple. If Microsoft was about functionality or feature, Apple was all about the experience. The Mac was friendly and much easier to use. It was a product that should have appealed to the NEO desire for the unique, the authentic and the experience...but there were problems.

Despite the design innovation and the emotional promise of the *1984* ad, there were fundamental issues that hadn't been addressed. The Mac's memory wasn't large enough for it to effectively run a lot of graphic programs, and it lacked a hard disc drive. Users had to use an external drive for storage. In other words, it was far easier to use than a PC, but you couldn't do much with it. To quote Adams again, "The Mac started out as a wonderfully simple and elegant idea (give them so little memory that they won't be able to do anything anyway)." That meant, despite piquing enormous interest, the product did not deliver the experience that would have thrilled the potential NEO audience and taken it beyond those few NEO-dominated professions in which Apple was already the preferred choice.

A year after its Superbowl splash, Apple was in deep trouble. In January 1985 it aired another Superbowl ad, "Lemmings," promoting the upcoming Macintosh Office, a direct attempt to challenge IBM. The ad revisited the idea that Apple's competitors were grey, unthinking drones. It bombed. Four months later the company was ruptured by a power struggle, when Jobs unsuccessfully attempted a coup against John Sculley, the man he had persuaded to take on the job of Apple president and CEO just two years earlier. Having tried his hand and lost, Jobs was stripped of his power, given the meaningless title 'Global Thinker' and moved to an office so remote it was nicknamed Siberia. To put it in terms we have been hearing a great deal in recent years, 'the adults were back in charge'.

They didn't do too well, though. Sculley had come to Apple from Pepsi-Cola, where he had been vice-president and had created the Pepsi Challenge. Although he is much maligned in the standard versions of the Apple story, his actions make perfect sense viewed through the prism of the Two Planets. This was the ultimate Traditional takeover of a struggling NEO company.

Sculley, a graduate of Wharton, had learned very well the business methods of Traditional Capitalism, and had effectively employed them during his time at PepsiCo. It is, of course, a company built on a product that is mostly reliant upon brand and distribution—in Two Planet terms, a text book commodity. It's not surprising, then, that at Apple Sculley followed the playbook of the Traditional economy and threw every available dollar at advertising as well as offering incentives to buy. In doing so, he effectively starved research and development and the things that made Apple unique.

He was simply doing what he knew best, and what he knew had worked elsewhere. He was applying a strategy effective with Traditionals or with a commoditized product (such as carbonated drinks) chosen on a matrix of status, features and price. That iconic *1984* ad created a brilliant brand halo – but the Mac didn't deliver. Had Sculley understood that experience outweighs brands for NEOs (who love to follow the whispered secret and discover things for themselves), he might have starved advertising and thrown everything the company had on research and development to ensure that next time the technology was in place.

Fortunately for Apple, Jean-Louis Gassée, head of research and development, had his own ideas about what should be done, and he had the clout to carry them off. He was one of the few people in the company who could and would stand up to Jobs. Sculley might have been at the helm, but Gassée had the respect of the company's designers and engineers, and that brought with it a different sort of power. Gassée understood them, and they understood him. Even more importantly, his principles were aligned with what NEOs value. While Sculley fretted over the high prices Apple charged because it had no lower-cost alternative, Gassée believed that the design features justified that higher price. Gassée wasn't interested in going after the mass market--his focus was on unique products with high-profit margins. It's true that many of Gassée's projects never saw the light of day, but even so, while Steve Job's would eventually rise again as 'the man who saved Apple,' it was Gassée who made sure that there was something left to save.

The struggles that unfolded between Sculley and Gassée were, in effect, a tug-of-war between the old world and the emerging world – between a Traditional, wanting to build a brand and offer a great deal to attract the largest numbers of buyers, and a NEO, who isn't interested in selling to everyone, only to those who could appreciate the product's difference and see the price as worth it. It is a struggle that is repeated every single day in companies all across the world, as NEOs and Traditionals try to impose their own worldviews. We can only wonder what might have happened if Sculley had been able to pursue his favored strategy and built lower-priced, more feature-rich products for the mass market. In doing so he would have erased everything that kept the company aligned with the NEOs and Evolvers who were on their way to becoming its customer base.

Sculley would stay at Apple until 1993, but the world was rapidly changing around him. NEOs had not yet become a dominant force in either the workplace or society in general, but the ground had been laid. 'Remote working' is an example of the kind of thing that hastened the emergence of the economic influence of NEOs and was made possible in the first place by their existence: the Virtuous Cycle at work.

Remote work is such a given now that there are shelves of books and hundreds of experts whose sole topic is how not to let work seep into every waking moment. But in the late 1980s, remote working was a breakthrough. It suited people who were at managerial level as well as the newly termed 'knowledge workers'--those who were employed because of what they could do, not because of where they could do it from.

Unlike the factory hands who powered the industrial revolution, this new breed, these knowledge workers, had the capacity to be just as productive at home or even on the move. But to realize that capacity they needed mobile computers that were compatible with the systems that they used at work. By 1989 the Mac Portable was ready to ship, but it was so big and bulky that it quickly earned the unflattering moniker 'the Luggable'. Its size made it too big to use on an airplane tray table, which is where many roaming workers wanted to take advantage of otherwise dead time.

Again, when it mattered, Apple had failed to deliver on the experience. But even this wasn't the company's biggest problem. The reality was that even if the Mac Portable had been a great product, it might not have sold well, thanks to the fact that at the time virtually every corporate technology decision was made by a small cadre of 'tech experts' rather than by the people who would be actually using the equipment. This fostered the corporate conservatism that led to the truism, "Nobody ever got fired for buying IBM." The people approving the purchasing decisions were usually Traditionals (and in many corporations they still are).

In 1990 came the announcement that Microsoft was partnering with Intel. This was a serious problem for Apple. It threatened to put Microsoft so far out of reach that Apple might never quite catch up. Certain that the company had to take drastic action, Sculley finally won his battle for a less costly product. The early effects of globalization meant that by now Apple could make computers much more cheaply. So it was able to launch the Mac Classic at the unprecedented low cost of $999 in October that year.

From here on, Apple had the pricing profile we all know and accept: above other computers on the market but still within reach of both NEOs and Evolvers as they joined the workforce and developed their economic power. But Apple still wasn't able to totally deliver the experience it promised. Other players had caught up, and although Apples were far easier to use, the sales team struggled to justify the higher price simply on the grounds of differentiation and user-friendliness.

In 1991, Apple made forced layoffs and hooked up with IBM in a deal that mimicked the arrangement between Microsoft and Intel. That same year, it launched its PowerBook. This proved a winning product—but not in the way Apple predicted. The PowerBook came in three versions, a lower-cost stripped-down version, a mid-range option, and the top of the range 170 that cost more than $4,000. Expecting to sell far more of the least expensive version, it was this Apple stocked up on, only to be faced with such strong demand for the 170 that it had a six-month backlog of orders.

Projecting demand for products of any kind is notoriously difficult. These projections are underpinned by assumptions about customers, and if you're wrong in your fundamental assumptions, you're going to be very wrong with your projections. Apple no doubt believed it would sell many more of the cheaper models because its assumptions were based on Traditional patterns of consumption. But it wasn't Traditionals who were buying the PowerBook. Had Apple recognized the existence of NEOs as an economic force and had understood how aligned it was to NEO values, it would have correctly predicted the greatest sales in the top of the range version, which offered a much better experience for its much higher price.

Decisions such as the one Apple made can be fatal, especially in an industry where speed is of the essence. There were repercussions, but again Apple avoided the worst outcomes. However, consistently disastrous sales culminated in 1993 in yet another coup, with John Sculley ousted in favor of the company's COO, Michael Spindler, who was far more prepared to take unpopular austerity measures to cut company costs. Further layoffs ensued and many of the perks that had buoyed Apple's workforce through the endless rounds of '90 hours a week and loving it' big pushes were also cut, leading to a drop in morale.

In terms of delivering experience, Apple was even closer to the mark with its 1994 Power Mac. As a result, sales rocketed--despite the fact that a design flaw meant that some literally burst into flames! But in one more bewildering misstep, the company appeared to seriously underestimate the impact of the internet, dragging its heels on the necessary preparations. The flow-on effect was that companies such as AOL took a further six months to develop Apple-compatible features, giving PCs the clear lead in the online revolution.

Worse was yet to come, with the launch of Microsoft's Windows '95. Competing Operating Systems were the centre of the battles for technological supremacy among computer companies, and with his 1995 release it seemed Bill Gates might have won the war. Apple was the tech leader in the creative industries, but that was a small slice of the corporate world and the rest was still run along Traditional lines and dominated by Traditional values. Windows '95 ticked Traditional boxes of status (Microsoft was the dominant brand), a host of new features and was offered in a complete package that made it a very good deal. It ensured that Microsoft was still the only real choice for corporations. Despite the major PR offensive Apple launched-- bombarding influential journalists with testimonials and lists of reasons why Apple was better--Windows 95 equaled market domination for Microsoft.

Apple suffered. New orders dried up, losses compounded (around that time, it had $1 billion worth of existing orders it couldn't meet) and more layoffs had to be made. The company was still trying to innovate, experimenting with touch-screen technology and launching its PDA, but (again) the technology to underwrite the experience wasn't quite there yet and the PDA bombed. Rumors of a corporate takeover of the company abounded.

In 1996, when Apple was just three months away from running out of funds altogether, Spindler was, in turn, ousted and Gil Amelio was appointed as CEO. Amelio, the CEO of National Semiconductor and a member of the Apple board, clearly shared Gassée's NEO worldview that people would pay extra for extra value, even if all the elements of the Virtuous Cycle weren't yet quite in place. But Apple had dropped so far behind the fast-paced technology race it was hard to see how it could catch up.

For people using computers supplied by their employers, system compatibility was a key issue. Design studios everywhere were full of Macs, and some NEOs were prepared to buy them for personal use, but the retail computing sector was nothing as important then as it has become. Profits came from the corporate sector, and when it came to work—and particularly remote work—what was needed was equipment compatible with the office. That meant choosing PC. Sales declined and Apple entered a downward spiral that could easily have become a death spin. Fewer of its computers selling meant a smaller potential market for the developers who were writing software, which in turn meant that less Apple-compatible software was written, which meant that you could do less on an Apple, which resulting in a further drop in sales.

In 1996, Apple posted a $69 million loss. It also bought NeXT, (the company that Jobs had gone off and formed when he was ousted by Sculley) in the hope that incorporating its operating system would give Apple the edge it needed to compete with Microsoft. Steve Jobs returned, initially in the role of consultant/advisor, but the following year he took back the position of CEO of Apple. He announced a new ethos, what came to be called co-operative competition with Microsoft; he was aiming for a world where everyone could be a winner. All he asked of the Apple team was that they focus on what had made Apple outstanding in the first place.

Jobs killed all the expensive, drawn out research and development projects that were going nowhere and put the resources into those projects within areas where they were already leaders–design and publishing. He put a new, strong focus on 'the experience'. The NEO who had started it all was back at the helm and the changes he made put the company back in alignment with NEOs, just as the New Economic Order started to flex its commercial power.

Jobs was helped immeasurably by the fact that the Virtuous Cycle was now in full force, giving Apple the best conditions for success. The price-crushing effect of globalization was in place, dropping the cost of production and effectively flattening the playing field. With the pressures of the cost of production eased, the NEO culture of Apple was able to concentrate more effectively on being unique and on the experience it was offering. The demographic effect meant that by this time sufficient numbers of NEOs were in the workforce and so were able to flex their economic muscle. The development of the web allowed easy, undiluted dissemination of communication from one Apple fanatic to another. And decision-making about computer purchases became more and more an individual, not corporate, as more and more people became consultants and entrepreneurs.

Now all Apple had to do was deliver on its promise of an outstanding experience and keep abreast of the edge it had secured by continuing to turn out new products that would appeal to NEOs. This time, it succeeded. Apple was able to turn the tide because, at the critical time, it (again) had at its helm a NEO who was able to align the company with the things that NEOs who bought its products value--most importantly, the place of design in the overall experience. From the early blue iMacs to the stunning iPad2, ever since Jobs' returned, Apple has produced objects that give NEOs a sense of personal expression just by having them in their space. It is important to understand that it is not the customers that changed; the values and attitudes that drive their purchase decisions are remarkably consistent. Rather, it was Apple's ability to catch up with them, to deliver unique products and experience, which underlies its success.

Can we really be so confident that Apple's success is mainly down to NEOs and Evolvers? In April 2012, the research company that we use, Roy Morgan Research Ltd., asked a pool of our participants which operating system they used. Of those who were asked, three times as many NEOs as Traditionals said that they used Apple. We also asked how many Apple products they owned. The results showed that the numbers are very similar in terms of the NEOs and Traditionals that owned one product, but when we asked who owned more than one, and then more than three Apple products, the difference between the types became startling. In fact, NEOs are eleven times more likely to own more than three Apple products than Traditionals. In other words, Traditionals do buy Apple products, but not as many NEOs and Evolvers by a long chalk.

It's important to remember that when the experience isn't there, neither are the NEO customers, however. The first Apple TV bombed, and reviews and sales of the original MacBook Air were both poor. Blind brand loyalty is a fiction when it comes to NEOs. If they don't judge the product to be worth it, no amount of brand building will persuade them otherwise.

For those alert to the changes, things have moved so fast that it's hard to believe that as recently as twenty years ago, Traditionals dominated the marketplace and Traditional thinking dominated business theory. Despite the changing landscape, for too many people the old way is the only way. That explains why the knee-jerk response from a business in trouble or one that wants to grab market share has been to build brands and cut prices--exactly as John Sculley wanted to do with Apple.

That approach can still work if a business can use economies of scale to offer extraordinary deals, and if its product is a commodity. But the hard lesson learned by Apple under Sculley, and by workers in manufacturing plants all over America which tried to retain jobs by cutting costs only to lose them to a new piece of technology or even cheaper labor elsewhere, is that you can't survive long term if all you have to offer is the second-best deal on Planet Traditional.

But this is about more than just deciding what strategy is going to get you through the recession or even the next five years. Whether they do it by accident or by design, businesses that succeed will be those that cater for the inhabitants of either of the Two Planets. It will become more and more crucial to business survival to avoid the vacuum in between because, as the Virtuous Cycle rolls on, that dead space will get ever wider.

The only thing that can stop this is if globalization goes away, or if modern technology disappears and if the NEOs and Evolvers start getting younger. That's not going to happen. Instead, NEOs will continue to exert more and more power. In ten years time, they'll dominate every adult age category under 60. The New Economic Order is the future, and for those able to meet its challenges, it is the opportunity of a lifetime.

As the Virtuous Cycle continues to turn and build even more momentum, it is pushing NEOs and Traditionals further and further apart. This doesn't mean a NEO son can't communicate with their Traditional father, or that neighbors can't be friendly across the divide between their two planets, but it terms of their behavior as consumers, the chalk is getting chalkier and the cheese cheesier. There are leading edge businesses on both planets, but the edge is always moving, driven further and further outwards by this increasing polarization.

Having regained its place at the edge after Steve Jobs' return, one of the reasons Apple has maintained it is that the enormous R&D and engineering requirements for anyone wishing to compete means that most choose to do so on the basis of brand, features and price, rather than by creating a product whose overall experience outdoes Apple's. Unwittingly, these competitors are positioning themselves in the dangerous middle ground—what they're offering is not compelling for NEOs, leaving them only with the lower margins from Traditionals and some compromising Evolvers This is not the place to be for long-term success (as Research In Motion seems to be finding out every week with its Blackberry lines).

Jobs acted instinctively when he returned to the flailing company and pushed it right out to the edge, where the NEOs were waiting. He didn't know he was a NEO any more than John Sculley knew he was a Traditional, pushing the company towards Traditional values. The real question for Apple now is, will new leader Tim Cook keep it at the edge and continue its success? If he's wise, he'll keep the NEOs on his team close and pay attention to what they say.

Ironically despite the importance of this economic extremism in Apple's success, the profile it has built means that it is increasingly the "safe" choice, which explains the number of Traditionals who buy Apple products. Having an iPod, iPhone or even an iPad is no longer as obvious a NEO indicator as it once was, because the status element of the deal appeals to more and more residents of the other planet. This is not too much of a problem for Apple, because it creates products that are in a state of constant evolution, pushing back the edge of what is possible, unique and new. It did, however, prove to be a big problem for one of the other biggest and most recognizable names in American business, Starbucks.

Like Apple, Starbucks is a relatively young company, having also been founded in the 1970s. Like Apple, its driving force was a NEO who built a huge success by working on gut instinct. Like Apple, it badly lost its way, and then got back to first principles. But the reason Starbucks got so far into dangerous territory, and the way it tried to correct its mistakes, reveals very different things about how to survive in the new Two Planet universe. That's a whole other story.

CHAPTER SIX
SLIDING TOWARDS THE MIDDLE
THE STARBUCKS STORY

S tarbucks is an American success story. From humble start-up to international powerhouse, it has redefined the way people the world over think about, talk about and drink coffee. Along its journey from the narrow streets of Pike Place Market in Seattle to what it is today, it has reaped the benefits and courted the dangers of the Two Planets. In fact, it demonstrates perhaps better than any other company the inherent conflict between Traditional 'good business' thinking and the drivers of the NEO Economy. Order yourself a skinny caramel macchiato and settle in for a cautionary tale.

In North America if there is some place you can buy a well-made espresso near where you live, work or shop, it's thanks in part to Howard Schultz, a man whose ambition was to put a decent cup of coffee within reach of everyone in the developed world.

It all began in 1971, when Gerald (Jerry) Baldwin, Zev Siegl, and Gordon Bowker were inspired by a Dutch immigrant called Alfred Peet, who ran a specialist coffee business in Berkeley, California. They opened their own store in Seattle's Pike Place Market district and called it Starbucks. It was not Starbucks as we know it, serving beverages. Instead, they roasted and sold the best coffee beans they could source, plus the equipment needed to make a great cup of coffee at home.

There is little doubt that Baldwin, Siegl, and Bowker (and Peet) were NEOs or Evolvers. in his book *Pour Your Heart Into It: How Starbucks Built a Company One Cup at a Time,* Schultz writes about the trio's interests in "producing films, writing, broadcasting, classical music, gourmet cooking, good wine, and great coffee"—essentially a checklist of NEOs' interests, as our research pinpoints. As Schultz describes it, they weren't just businessmen; they were in some way also artisans, with the palates and sensitivities to appreciate the difference between the more expensive Arabica coffee beans favored by Europeans and the inferior but cheaper Robusta beans the majority of Americans were drinking at the time. Crucially, they also had a passionate conviction that given a choice, other Americans would respond as they did.

On paper there were many reasons Starbucks should not have succeeded. Across the U.S., coffee consumption was actually in decline; the big brands like Folgers and Maxwell House were hacking away at the quality of what was on sale in an attempt to maintain their profit margins. In diners, truck stops and bodegas alike, coffee was often referred to as "High Test," a phrase adapted from full-octane gasoline. Its purpose was to rev you up, not to taste good.

As well, in the early 1970s the whole of the Pacific Northwest, and Seattle in particular, was going through a deep, long-lasting recession. The area's big employer, Boeing, was suffering the ravages of the oil crisis, and the fishing and forestry industries were in decline. Standard business thinking would say that going into gourmet coffee roasting, the very definition of discretionary spending, at a time when unemployment is high and the economy is struggling is lunacy. But as Schultz observes, "the founders of Starbucks were not studying market trends. They were filling a need--their own need--for quality coffee."

Baldwin, Siegl, and Bowker were working on instinct, but looking back now through the Two Planet prism we can understand just why things played out the way they did. Given that the gravitational pull on each planet is now even stronger than it was back then, there is much in their story that can feed into 21st Century business success, for those who wish to see it.

Schultz describes it this way, "In the early 1970s, a few Americans, especially in the West Coast, were starting to turn away from prepackaged, flavor-added foods...Instead they chose to cook with fresh vegetables and fish, buy fresh-baked bread, and grind their own coffee beans. They rejected the artificial for the authentic...the mediocre for the high quality." That pattern of behavior and consumption is something we recognize as being deeply characteristic of NEOs. But rather than changing themselves, what Schultz observed was their economic emergence. These were people increasingly able to express their values through their spending. Schultz had witnessed a change "*of*" people, even though he interpreted it as a change "*in*" people.

Starting as it did in a recession, it is significant that the company was selling something not just strongly appealing to NEOs and Evolvers, but was at a price point within reach of both. They may not yet have been able to afford the house or car in their mind's eye, but their passion for new experiences and authenticity could be expressed on a small scale in this new temple to great coffee. It became a whispered secret, passed along from one experience-seeker to the next. Uber-NEO Howard Schultz was soon one of those in on the secret.

What separates NEOs from Traditionals are their different sets of values translated into behavior. To find out what people value you can look at what they do, but it's also useful to listen to what they say. When Schultz enthuses about those the things that really move him, it's clear he is drawn to experience, exploration, and discovery, to the unique and the authentic. This is what shines through as he recalls his first visit to Seattle and his immediate fascination with Starbucks and good coffee. Having served as a Xerox sales rep, he had moved on to the kitchen-equipment company Hammarplast, and it in this context that the New Yorker first visited Pike Place. 'I was," he recalls, "enamored. Here was a whole new culture before me, with knowledge to acquire and places to explore." Oh, so NEO.

Schultz's enchantment with coffee roasting became a career move—he joined Starbucks as Director of Retail Operations and Marketing. But it was a business trip to Milan that turned it into a lifelong love-affair. In Italy he visited espresso bars where he soaked up the atmosphere and sampled the daily 'theater' of coffee. It was a revelation. He decided that "Starbucks had missed the point...what we had to do was unlock the romance and mystery of coffee, first hand, in coffee bars."

He returned home convinced that the company simply *had* to recreate the entire authentic experience on to American soil. He attempted to win Starbucks' founders around to his idea, but they wanted to stick to what they were doing successfully. He persisted and finally they relented: in April 1984 Schultz was allocated 300 square feet in the next Starbucks set to open, the sixth. Within this downtown store he created his first espresso bar.

This was his moment. On the bar's first day, Schultz was thrilled to note that the store served 400 customers rather than the usual 250, and that "Customers jammed into the small space on the right whilst the retail counter stood empty." Word of mouth soon saw the numbers accelerate to 800 per day.

Emboldened by this success, yet unable to persuade the owners of Starbucks to jump in with both feet, he left the company intent on opening his own chain of authentic Italian-style coffee bars. He refined his ideas, drew up business plans and set out to drum up financial backing. He pitched his dream over and over again. Some got it straight away and wrote checks. Others, alarmed at his obsession, attempted to explain the errors in his thinking. One piece of feedback Schultz recalls: 'Americans are never going to spend a dollar and a half for coffee.' It's easy to look back and laugh at that now, but that quote contains a wealth of useful insight about the importance in business of understanding who you are talking to.

When people talk that way, what they usually mean is *'I* wouldn't spend a dollar and a half for coffee.' Attempting to sound more convincing, they may say, 'The average consumer wouldn't spend a dollar and a half for coffee'. If that's true at all, it's only because there is *no such thing as an average consumer.*

From the outset Schultz was pitching a NEO concept (although that name did not yet exist). He was attempting to create a business that relied on customers happily paying a premium for something unique, individual, authentic and extraordinary. But try pitching this to a Traditional investor, hard-wired to think in terms of status, feature or deal. Trying to persuade someone of something so at odds with their own values is as fruitless as expecting a racehorse to appreciate poetry. If we could have spoken to the young Howard Schultz, we would have said, "Give up on changing people's minds. Instead align with those who care about the same things you do, there are plenty of them."

It's not surprising Schultz met a lot of rejection and incomprehension. He was attempting something radical. He was trying to de-commoditize coffee, one of the most commoditized products in world. The first investor was the employer he had just left. Starbucks handed over a big-hearted $15,000, saying that, although they felt they couldn't follow his lead, they supported what he was doing. But it was a drop in the ocean. Schultz needed to raise $400,000 in seed capital and a further $1.25 million to realize his intention of opening eight stores.

Right from the start, he was determined to launch a 'major enterprise, not just a single store'. In fact, the number of envisioned stores rose and rose. At first, he wanted 50 stores in five years. That aim soon became 75 stores in five years and then 125 stores in five years. Of course, those figures were dwarfed by the number of stores Starbucks would go on to open, but the grand-scale vision was there from the start.

That ambition would prove to be very significant in the way Starbucks developed. In order to fund such big plans, Schultz had to give away far more of the business than he would have liked. It also meant that he had an externally driven profit schedule – he may have been focused on the romance of the Grande Latte, but his investors simply wanted timely financial returns. This would create a dangerous tension between Schultz's commitment to the unique and individual and Traditional Capitalism's inherent demands.

Schultz opened his first store in April 1986. Concerns that Il Giornale, the name he had chosen inspired by a Milanese newspaper, was too foreign and hard to pronounce evaporated as he discovered that his customers "took pride in the way they said it, as though they were part of a club." (Complexities don't deter NEOs, they delight them.)

Il Giornale was lovingly modeled along traditional Italian lines, and within six months the first store was serving 1,000 customers a day. Schultz' instincts had paid off. As with Apple, his company was unwittingly boosted by changes in the way people worked: increasingly mobile, they wanted somewhere to sit and be productive that was neither home nor office. For Seattleites, Il Giornale had become what is now known as 'the third place'. And unlike Apple in its early days, Schultz wasn't waiting for the technology to catch up—he could deliver on his promise to customers, day in, day out. When you stepped in to one of his coffee bars you were offered a range of new experiences, from the smell of the roasted beans, to language that enabled you to create a drink exactly as you wanted it. Individualism ruled.

In 1987, the founders of Starbucks decided that they wanted to go their separate ways. Schultz raised more money and bought the company, including the rights to the name. The Starbucks Corporation was born and the existing coffee bars were renamed.

As the company grew, Schultz paid close attention to each store's most important assets: the quality of beans and the highly trained baristas, central players in the 'theater of coffee'. He took care of all the employees, giving even part-time workers full health coverage and later 'Beanstock' stock options. His company has always been progressive, especially on issues of sustainability and how it treats its workers, a fact that is too easy to forget for those who see it only as a huge multinational empire.

Starbucks continued to expand and Schultz is justified in his pride in the skill needed to select the right locations. The choices were informed by insights yielded by the successful mail order business the original Starbucks had run, which showed that the typical Starbucks catalogue customer was 'a connoisseur, highly educated, relatively affluent, well-travelled and technologically savvy, with a significant interest in the arts and other cultural events'. We couldn't have described NEOs better ourselves.

Eventually Starbucks built to the point where it was opening 365 new stores annually—one for every day of the year, a feat made possible in part by buying out existing chains and rebranded them. The logistics are breathtaking; however the company attempted to learn from every mistake along the way and refined the process until it had it down pat. Starbucks was a growth machine. But the fault lines started to show.

In order to make things happen so fast, design decisions were made that effectively homogenized the stores as they rolled out across America. If you are opening a store a day, there simply isn't time to arrive at a bespoke design for every single location. Opening coffee bars is very capital-intensive undertaking, so leveraging economies of scale by buying fixtures and fittings in bulk must have seemed like a no-brainer.

Unfortunately, this is a critical point of conflict between the cost-based Traditional economy and the growing NEO one. The sense of place, or provenance, doesn't show up on the balance sheet, but for a company that appeals to NEOs, it is often the most valuable part of the business.

To his great credit Schultz recognized it as an issue. Starbucks arrived at a compromise solution that involved minor variations in the final look of each store. But compromises are not the currency of Planet NEO. Homogeneity, however much you try to disguise it, cannot co-exist with the unique. The decision to opt for speedy expansion at the cost of bespoke tailoring for each new location would imperil the company in the years ahead.

Starbucks went public in 1992 and, in 1994, realizing it was not physically possible for him to continue to oversee every aspect of a company that was now 500 stores large, Schultz and the board promoted Orin Smith to president and chief operating officer in 1994. This ostensibly to free up Schultz, who was still chairman and CEO, to "continue to create the vision, to anticipate the future, to experiment with creative ideas."

Smith was a talented businessman and a safe hand at the helm; Schultz, however, had become a danger to the company he loved. Always alive to possibilities for innovation and expansion, he set out to stretch the brand far beyond the offerings found in traditional coffee bars, creating a Starbucks-branded jazz CD (*Blue Note Blend*); coffee ale; frozen Frappuccino's, and then, in collaboration with Pepsi, bottled Frappuccino; and Starbucks own coffee ice cream, with the latter two products selling through supermarkets.

He was trying to cement his company as 'best in class' for all coffee-related products. But while these developments were commercially successful, they weren't in line with his original aim of creating a theater for coffee consumption underpinned by a sense of community.

Schultz writes bitterly about the lack of understanding from market analysts, who suggested his focus might have strayed; he counters their criticism by pointing to the commercial success of many of the new products. But both Schultz and the analysts missed the point. The problem was not lack of focus, it was that the company's overall trajectory—both its chain expansion into so many new locations and its new product lines—eroded the authenticity of experience that had drawn the NEOs and Evolvers in the first place.

Still the company expanded, opening more stores in the U.S., spreading to other countries, and opening outlets in existing bookstores, supermarkets, and other chains. It was following the standard playbook for success--spot a gap in the market, raise funds, launch, expand, go global.

Starbucks began to seem ubiquitous; there was one on every corner and they all looked the same. The number of stores became a punch line on shows including *The Simpsons*. It started to appear like the McDonald's of coffee bars and it began to attract the same sort vociferous criticism about corporate-empire building. It was seen as a ruthless expander, crushing locally owned businesses as it went. It became fashionable in some quarters to loudly boycott the company, and in 1999 protests at a World Trade Organization meeting in Seattle descended into riots in which stores including Starbucks were targeted. The images made news around the world. To be seen as the embodiment of faceless corporate greed must have been a shocking slap in the face for a company that had begun so authentically and achieved so much. This rollercoaster ride from whispered NEO secret to vilification had taken just 15 years.

Again to his credit, Schultz was aware of a growing problem long before people started smashing up his stores, writing, "By 1995, the Starbucks brand faced an identity crisis...the field was getting so crowded that some customers couldn't differentiate us from scores of competitors. Distracted by our size and ubiquity, they missed the point about our quality and commitment to community. The key threat to the Starbucks brand was a growing belief amongst customers that the company was becoming corporate and predictable, inaccessible, or irrelevant."

He was in the right ballpark, but using the Two Planet prism we can see that the problem was not quite the way Schultz defined it. It wasn't that "customers" in general were turning away as a result of Starbuck's size and ubiquity. Those very things reassured Traditionals, who place a higher value upon safety when they spend. However, the company's changing profile was certainly off putting for NEOs and Evolvers, who have an inbuilt mistrust of large Organizations. Far from the early experience of NEOs thrilled to stumble across a new Starbucks in their neighborhood, they now couldn't get away from them

Ubiquity isn't just about how many stores you have. It's also about how many other places you're seen in. When Starbucks launched, Schultz had decided against selling its beans through supermarkets, wanting to maintain "a clear distinction from grocery store coffee." With bottled Frappucino and ice cream, the company had broken its own rule. Then in 1996, United Airlines started serving Starbucks coffee.

Standard business thinking would say this was a great move, as long as you accounted for risks such as the known difficulty of maintaining quality in food or beverage consumed at high altitudes. (Before the coffee started selling onboard, Schultz had satisfied himself that any problems in quality had been solved.) Certainly, the United deal was the kind of business decision you'd make if you wanted to hit some really big figures, especially if you were worried about the effect of competitors on your margin. And by this time, Starbucks did have competition. Ironically, it now faced a proliferation of independent coffee houses and rival chains opening in its wake and drawing away the very customers whose enthusiasm had enabled it to get so big.

Starbucks' vulnerability to competitors was the polar opposite to Apple's. As we've noted, Apple maintains its position at the outer edge of Planet NEO because its competitors focus on features, brand, or pricing rather than matching the overall experience. In other words, they commoditize themselves. For Starbucks, the risk came not from one big company challenging and besting it. Its Achilles heel proved to be small, independent coffee bars, especially in areas with high concentrations of NEOs and Evolvers. Despite its solid-gold NEO pedigree, it is remarkably easy to out-NEO at a local level. Intelligentsia in LA, Octane Coffee in Atlanta, Ninth Street Espresso in New York, and thousands of other independent stores across the country do precisely this. For them, Starbucks is no threat. Free from prescriptive brand parameters, they can be unique, extraordinary, and appealing to the NEO love of discovery and provenance. As independents, each has a free hand in decisions about the decor and the menu (including how often it changes) and each can source its own beans.

As the 20th anniversary of its founding approached in 2004, NEOs and Evolvers hadn't deserted Starbucks—in fact, they still dominated its turnover, even though they were increasingly being pulled towards those independent competitors. The reason for this seeming paradox is simple: NEOs eat and drink out more often, and spend more each time they do. This is an undeniable fact—easily seen in the decades' worth of data we've examined—but it's all too easy to miss if your analysis centers on the "average spend" by the (mythical) "average customer."

To see how this works, imagine a Starbucks counter. Lined up are ten customers who spend a total of $40. That's an average of $4 each. Look again, through the Two Planet prism. Four of those customers are Traditionals, stopping by to spend $1.50 on a black coffee. The other six are NEOs, here to buy cappuccinos, a few sandwiches, and a biscotti or two, for an average spend of more than $5 each.

Looking at the entire line as if they were all one type of customer gives you a very misleading picture. It's true that in strictly mathematical terms, the average spend in that line is $4. But if you fail to differentiate between the NEOs and the Traditionals, the accuracy of your averaging ability is all you have to comfort you when your business starts to wobble.

What about if, rather than average spend, you looked at which products were up and which were down? Perhaps such an analysis reveals that drinks sales are stable, but sales of food are declining. The marketing playbook says you should start offering "package" deals, tying a food purchase to a drink for an overall price saving to the customer. But this is just as useless as average spend data unless you know which of the Two Planets you are on.

Is your business aimed at Traditionals? Great, package away (just don't assume they will still be there when normal prices kick back in—their loyalty is first and foremost to the deal). But if it's NEOs you're targeting, forget it, that's not what will draw them in. If you have a mixed customer base and you respond to falling sales with package deals, you are turning cartwheels for your lowest-value customers, and overlooking the things you could to appeal to your highest-value customers, the NEOs.

So what could you do instead? Our recent round of research completed in April, 2012, showed that NEOs are eight times more likely than Traditionals to visit a specialty coffee store five times or more in a week and six times more likely to spend between $6 and $9 when they do. So here is what you wouldn't do: You wouldn't offer them a discount. Instead, you'd improve and evolve their experience. Knowing that NEOs like to try new things and love the process of discovery, you could vary the menu, adding choices based on their provenance or uniqueness. And keep changing it. Because even if you sell the most incredible sandwich made from locally baked artisan bread, hand-made organic cheese, and rucola grown in your roof garden, at some point, whether it's after a week or a year, the NEOs who frequent your store are going to want to eat something different. What makes you unique this week?

If only Starbucks management had understood this. Instead, they set about re-commoditizing their offering.

In 2005, Orin Smith retired. The title of CEO passed to Jim Donald. It was the kind of appointment that satisfies 'the market' because Donald had cut his teeth at discount chains such as Wal-Mart and Pathmark Stores (where he'd been chairman, president and CEO) and he brought with him a reputation for turning around the ailing fortunes of chains. By the end of that year, Starbucks had expanded to 10,241 stores. That growth is astonishing enough in two decades, but Donald announced that Starbucks planned to open a staggering 40,000 more stores worldwide. It was classic Traditional business strategy, where bigger is always better and the concept of 'world class' is highly appealing. But Donald quickly found himself under siege.

In 2006, in a direct attack on Starbucks, McDonald's began serving premium coffee. Commentators understood that there was a threat—even if they didn't really understand the nature of it. The way one business journalist called it, "white-collar customers were leaving Starbucks for the independents, while blue-collar customers were opting for the fast food chain for their coffee." Of course, as you can now see, it had nothing to do with the color of their collars; it was about their deeply held values.

It's true that in many locations, Starbucks remained the most viable choice for many NEOs, Evolvers, and some Traditionals. Take, for example, a NEO waiting at an airport with three choices for her coffee. One is Starbucks, the second is a Cinnabon, franchise and the third is McDonald's. This is essentially a 'forced choice' landscape, and, given that there is simply no authentic or extraordinary option, it's highly likely this NEO would be drawn back to Starbucks over the other options. Traditionals however would be split between the three options. Those who liked the status and safety of the brand would be in Starbucks, whereas those driven by the deal would likely choose

McDonald's ("Why pay more?"). Some would go to Cinnabon, because "it's just coffee."

But Starbucks' figures showed it had begun to lose customers (not overall—more stores meant more customers as a total, but per-store figures were down) and their "average spend" had dropped. Like many businesses, the company's fortunes wax and wane around small shifts in overall percentages. A drop in growth from three percent to one percent was enough to galvanize it into extraordinary action. It instigated decisions that adversely affected the quality of the experience itself. In his second book *Onward: How Starbucks Fought for Its Life without Losing Its Soul*, Schultz detailed how he thought Jim Donald's single-minded focus on growth undermined the customer experience.

First, rapid expansion brought with it rapid turnover of store managers. That made it harder to keep the quality of the experience within a given store high, and it was almost impossible to build the relationship with repeat customers that had been a feature then the company was smaller. Again, this is all about the vastly different perspectives between NEOs and Traditionals.

Traditional companies believe, with some justification, that the customer has a relationship with the brand and the stronger the brand, the stronger the relationship. But what they fail to understand is that the most valuable customers, NEOs, distrust large corporations and faceless institutions, but they do trust individuals. (This is true even when those individuals are at the head of a large corporation. For many NEOs, Yvon Chouinard at Patagonia or Apple's Steve Jobs are judged trustworthy because of perceived shared values.) Even if the coffee store is part of a chain, when a NEO is welcomed each morning by name and offered 'their usual' drink it builds a relationship they value. That might extend to feeling more positively about the chain, but even so, the relationship is with the person behind the counter, not the company they work for. When the employee moves on to a new store, the relationship is lost.

The second problem was that the beans were being shipped and stored in vacuum packs. When Il Giornale opened, it was still legal to smoke in eateries but Schultz banned it in his cafes because he didn't want anything to interfere with the experience of drinking coffee. He thought it vital that the seductive aroma of freshly roasted and ground beans be allowed to work their olfactory magic on customers and passers-by. Now, stored in vacuum packs, the fragrance was locked away.

Third, the company had introduced semi-automated espresso machines, meaning that the baristas were increasingly partially obscured operatives, rather than the main actors in the everyday theater of coffee. To those who value experience and authenticity, Starbucks was systematically ridding itself of the very elements that had made Schultz and millions of NEOs and Evolvers fall in love.

There is no doubt that Jim Donald thought he was doing the best for the company—he was doing precisely the kinds of things he had done elsewhere to great effect. But it wasn't the right approach for Starbucks. As had happened at Apple, it was a clash of the Planets, a mismatch of leader and enterprise, bound to see one or the other go under. (When a founder moves aside from the company they have grown from scratch, the clamor is always for someone with 'experience,' who is 'acceptable to the market,' completely ignoring the fact that neither Jobs nor Schultz, nor dozens more like them, had the superstar *résumés* when they built their companies in the first place!)

As its growth flattened to one percent, Starbucks was in real danger of stagnating or commencing a serious decline. Realizing he had to do something drastic, in 2008 Schultz made the difficult decision to remove Jim Donald and return as Starbucks' CEO and president. Publicly acknowledging that the company's enormous expansion plan and its recent decisions had worked to its detriment, Schultz promised shareholders, staff, the media, and customers that he had would fix things by pulling the focus back to the theatre and romance of coffee.

In *Onwards*, he describes his realization that what the company needed to do was 'advance its position as the undisputed coffee authority.' This is significantly different to his earlier goal of becoming 'best in class' for *all coffee-related products*. Schultz decided his team had to curtail growth to a level that allowed them to sustain this goal. They had to switch focus from being a global company to "a company that made great coffee, one cup at a time."

In many ways Schultz's declaration should serve as the manifesto of the NEO Economy. When growth alone is the goal, it's too easy to make compromises that can undermine the long-term sustainability of the business. The alternative is to target growth in combination with an understanding of your customers' values. That way, your decisions serve to make your business the most valuable it can be.

Again, it may initially seem contradictory, but NEOs' mistrust of big companies only kicks in when they feel they are not being treated as an individual. NEOs are very happy to support Apple, Patagonia, and Anthropologie. They're not thinking about whether the store they're standing in is number one or number 701 in the company's history, because each store feels unique and anchored in its place. NEO-targeted companies are, in effect, servicing 113 million markets of one; they have no use for the Traditional Capitalism playbook.

Soon after his return, Schultz made the bold move of closing every single store for three hours to retrain all the company's baristas. Next, he permanently shut down 600 underperforming stores across America. Most of them had been recently opened near existing stores, in an effort to cut waiting times. Instead, they had simply cannibalized existing customers and reduced each store's profits thanks to those costly overheads.

He also removed hot food items from the menu and other irrelevant items such as soft toys that were being sold in some stores. The company reverted to transporting and storing beans in sacks, and ensured the grinding took place on the premises so the stores once again had the distinct, seductive aroma of coffee.

At one point, Schultz recalls a conversation with an ad agency in which he observed, "We're being squeezed from the bottom by fast food brands like McDonald's and Dunkin' Donuts, and from the top by high-end independent coffee shops...We have to make certain that we don't get caught in the middle." Reading this, we couldn't help but let out a cheer. Trusting his instinct once again, Schultz had sensed the dangerous vacuum between the Two Planets.

Another step he took to avoid being lost in this dead space was to try to 'de-brand' by opening the 15th Avenue Coffee and Tea store and nearby Roy Street Cafe in Seattle. This was a direct attempt to increase provenance and the uniqueness of each store, but it is hard to rewrite history and claim to be an independent again. Starbucks considered the stores "learning environments" but cynics quickly started referring to them both as "Fauxbucks." In July 2011 the 15th Avenue location reverted to the Starbucks brand.

More successful was the 2010 redesign and refurbishment of the Starbucks store in Olive Way, Seattle, using 'reclaimed and local materials' and featuring work from local artists. Along with the new look, the store introduced beer and wine and a wider selection of food. It's been successful enough that the company plans to roll out the concept in California, Atlanta, and Chicago, with each store tailored to its particular neighborhood.

It was clear that a NEO was back in charge, which was what the company needed. But there's no room for complacency.

The momentum created by the Virtuous Cycle means that the edges are constantly pushing further out and the gap between NEOs and Traditionals is getting ever bigger. What this means for Starbucks, and any other company that has lost and then regained its way, is that it isn't enough to restore the company to its former glory. The team in charge must be able to recognize where the edge now lies and stay ahead as that edge continues to shift.

There are many lessons to be drawn from the (ongoing) story of Schultz and Starbucks—specific dos and don'ts that can benefit anyone else running a business aimed at NEOs. But the story illustrates perfectly two absolute truths: the importance of understanding what is really driving your most valuable customers, and the fact that we urgently need to create new sources of capital. Sources which understand that, for businesses appealing to high-value NEOs and Evolvers, long-term value and sustainability is not created by pulling businesses towards the homogeneity and conformity of "going global." That instead, it comes from thinking small—not in scope, but in execution. With "113 million markets of one" in the US alone, the opportunity to build the connection with those who seek the edge, and are willing to pay for it, means the business you create is harder to replace, and ultimately more valuable.

Traditional capital works just fine for Traditional business ventures. But as Schultz and many other entrepreneurs found out, its demands can lead a NEO business down a dangerous road. To rebuild the American economy we don't need to replace capitalism, we need to expand it. NEO businesses need NEO Capital and NEO managers, who maximize value by ensuring that their company stays in alignment with the NEOs and Evolvers, rather than push them away by following a playbook that doesn't even recognize their existence.

CHAPTER SEVEN
HOW TO OUT-NEO A NEO

The road to business hell isn't just paved with good intentions; it's also strewn with the dust of promising start-ups. While it is incontrovertibly true that businesses which get it right and draw in free spending NEO customers are insulated against downturns in the wider economy, it's also true that even the most NEO of businesses will fall into a heap if they back away from the edge while their competitors are pushing out that edge as hard as they can. On Planet NEO it's not about which guy blinked, it's about which one stayed true to the core-deep values of the people buying their products.

Unfortunately, and ironically, one of the biggest threats to successful NEO businesses is that their success attracts investors and managers who seem to offer the chance to take that business to the next level and the one after that: to fulfill even the wildest ambitions of someone who has created something from nothing. But almost inevitably, the capital these investors are offering comes with strings, ways of doing things that are so familiar they seem standard, benign.

Benchmarking, consumer focus groups, market 'wisdom'—these are the basics of the Traditional model. But they're not benign. Indeed, for NEO businesses, they are toxic, as Harry Cragoe found out.

In the early 1990s Cragoe went from the UK to work for a while in Los Angeles, where he fell in love...with smoothies. Wholesome and delicious, the drinks he was soon buying on a daily basis weren't like any available near his home in England. There were, at the time, a small number of London stores that would blend smoothies to order, or you could buy your own blender and make one at home—a fiddly process with a mess to clean up afterwards. In California there were all manner of options on sale: exotic juice combos, protein shakes, dairy-based, dairy-free....They were only beverages, but to Harry Cragoe they represented a world of possibilities.

Returning to the UK, Cragoe sold everything he had in order to launch a smoothie business with his friend Patrick Folkes. Like the founders of Starbucks, they were working on gut instinct, believing that if they enjoyed the product so much, others would, too. An interview Cragoe gave to *The Times* of London in the days of the company captures an experience common to NEO entrepreneurs. In the piece he describes the incomprehension and lack of interest he met when trying to explain his idea, in this case to British fruit drink manufacturers, who simply couldn't see what was so wonderful about this new drink he wanted to create and who offered the opinion that there was no demand for 'things like that' in the UK. Cragoe's original desire to recreate the freshness and wholesomeness he had fallen for was thwarted by the stonewall response. Unable to get a local juice manufacturer on side, he and Folkes had to settle for shipping in from the U.S. frozen smoothies made from rehydrated fruit concentrates.

Next, came the question of what to call the company. The standard business playbook asserts that if you want to be successful, you have to build a successful brand. To do that, you need to decide what you want your brand identity to be, and then construct a company around it. Cragoe and Folkes wanted to launch something that brought a touch of the West Coast's fun and healthy lifestyle to the British market. They invented two characters, Pete and Johnny, photographed a pair of their friends who had the right look, and put them on their labels. The brand name quickly became shortened to PJ's.

PJ's launched in 1994 through Cullen's, an American supermarket chain that had moved into the UK. Despite it being twice the cost of other available fruit drinks at the time, sales swiftly began to build. Other companies followed with rival products, but by 2004 PJ's was the number one-selling smoothie in the UK.

Pepsi's acquisition of the company in 2005 was cause for huge celebration at PJ's. Cragoe's big gamble was paying off. PepsiCo is a major operation with an enormous amount of expertise and, crucially, wholesale and retail distribution that promises success for any growing company. This was being told as an extraordinary success story that could only continue. The future looked exceedingly bright.

Seen through the Two Planet prism, what Cragoe and Folkes had done was to launch a product that was (compared to anything else available at the time) extraordinary and unique. As well, the labels hinted at an intriguing back-story. Pete and Johnny suggested a West Coast version of Ben and Jerry, the ice cream mavens. If Ben and Jerry are the guys you'd like sit on the porch and watch the sunset with, Pete and Johnny were the kind of guys with whom you'd go surfing or mountain biking or do other cool, adventurous things. Or they would be, if they existed.

Although Cragoe and Folkes didn't recognize it in these terms, PJ's was a company that had begun by pushing the NEO edge and had found there lots of customers more than willing to pay its higher prices. By now it had competitors, but PJ's more closely aligned with what its NEO customers valued than anyone else in the UK smoothie market.

By all standard measures, 2008 should have been a good year for PJ's. A Mintel Research report put the value of the UK smoothie market that year at £282 million ($330 million), noting "increased household penetration" and "…people drinking smoothies more frequently throughout the day." (*Which* people, it didn't specify.) Yet, that was the year in which, following a 70 percent drop in sales and unsuccessful attempts to revive it, Pepsi decided to kill off PJ's. Today, if you manage to locate the PJ's website, you are greeted with only the logo and a sad, short message stating that it has 'retired'.

What happened?

In that same 2008 report, Mintel focused upon the competitive threat posed by "major brands" such as Pepsi-owned Tropicana which would launch a range of smoothies that same year. The (standard Traditional Capitalism) rationale is that it's the larger companies you have to watch out for, since they're the ones who can outdo new players on price, brand, and distribution. Of course this is true when you're talking about commoditized products, appealing to buyers with Traditional values. But it isn't true for NEO products, and PJ's was a NEO product. Had Mintel understood the NEO consumer, the Two Planet Principle, and the Virtuous Cycle, they wouldn't have got things so very wrong. The report made passing mention of another fledgling brand, Innocent Smoothies, but only to note that it faced the same competitive pressures as PJ's.

Pepsi became a global success by acquiring a portfolio of companies that produce drinks whose mix of brand, features, and price gives them enormous appeal to Traditionals (as well as to NEOs who are buying a commodity). Unsurprisingly, the company has developed a way of operating that it regards as a winning formula. It is a huge name on Planet Traditional. But that's the wrong planet for a NEO company like PJ's.

As PJ's was being killed off, Innocent Drinks was going from strength to strength. It had begun a decade earlier when three friends who worked in advertising and consultancy, Richard Reed, Jon Wright, and Adam Balon, decided to create something healthy for the kind of people they worked alongside--the kind they had been trained by their work to refer to as 'Young, Urban Professionals' or Yuppies.

The three friends played around with different flavors for six months, then spent £500 ($800) on fruit and took their best blends to sell at a London music festival. At the front of their stall they put two trashcans where customers could throw their empty cups, along with a sign asking, 'Should we give up our jobs to make these smoothies?' One trashcan was marked "Yes," the other "No." By the end of the festival, there were only three cups in the can marked "No." The "Yes" can was overflowing. Their decision was made for them.

PJ's Cragoe had returned from LA with an innate sense that if he liked smoothies and he was British, then there was a very good chance that other British people might like them too. (Hint--the British part is not the most important factor). Innocent also eschewed the usual market research route in favor of trying out their drinks on 'people like them'-- the people they hoped would buy them. (Now we're getting there.) Undoubtedly, the main reason for this would have been the cost involved plus the fact that, unlike a major corporation which would have run focus groups and test campaigns, they didn't have to justify their decisions to anyone. In retrospect, it's easy to see that this worked in all of their favor. Had the team from Innocent taken their blends into a focus group assembled on the basis of age, income, or some other factor they would have ended up with a mix of NEOs and Traditionals, and most likely a far more mixed response. If they'd set out a stall in an area frequented by a high number of Traditionals, even young ones, such as a suburban shopping mall, they might have found it hard to attract people to try the product and they would definitely have encountered a similar response to the one Howard Schulz got, that "people wouldn't pay" $3.50 for a cup of juice. But they didn't. Instead they went to a place where there was a high concentration of NEOs and Evolvers, and the seeds of their success were sown.

The founders of Innocent might have been trained to target Yuppies, but doing so could never have taken them to the level they went on to reach. Innocent found a much larger market than that. There are, undoubtedly, NEOS who are young, urban, and professional, but that covers just three defining markers. There are plenty of Yuppie Traditionals, too, and these people would probably have thought Innocent's founders were wasting their time and money. We use 184 measures to classify a NEO; that's what shows us so precisely how key values and attitudes translate into spending behavior. Once you've been able to see things in such precise detail, the crudeness of a descriptor like 'Yuppie' is almost painful. Hoping to predict consumer behavior armed only with concepts like 'Yuppie' is like trying to paint the Mona Lisa using a broom.

Innocent faced its own set of tough times at the start, but the men running it were far more unyielding in their approach than the founders of PJ's. The Innocent trio report being turned down by every bank they approached. This is not surprising—decision-makers in the bank and finance sector are trained to look at things through the prism of Traditional Capitalism. PJ's had already built 'the cool brand,' there was impending entry of massive international corporations who could crush this planned start-up, and these guys had never done this before. If you tick that many 'against' boxes, you don't get the money.

Reed, Wright, and Balon persisted, however, and endured a start-up period fraught with the long hours and rollercoaster of elation and despair that many new businesses go through. And it's at this point that Innocent Smoothie's story diverges from ultimately doomed start-ups such as PJ's. The Two Planets and the Virtuous Cycle started working in their favor. Unlike Howard Schulz, who had to make big compromises in how he built Starbucks in order to keep the capital rolling in, the young men at Innocent had a huge slice of luck. They made a presentation to U.S. businessman Maurice Pinto.

Pinto, who is also the Chairman of the UK's Ballet Black, which gives dancers of African and Asian descent opportunities within classical ballet, was not your typical investor. Previously he had put money into in an eclectic range of firms including Christy's Hats, a 250-year-old company that was mainly a supplier to the equestrian set. By the time he sold his investment, Christy's had become a cultural and fashion icon, selling stylish fedoras, caps, Trilbies, and duckbills, and running a successful online store. By becoming unique and design-focused, the company rooted in the past became a contemporary success. When Pinto sold his share to the management, it was for seven times his original investment.

In the book *Innocent, Building a Brand from Nothing but Fruit*, author John Simmons interviewed Pinto to find out why he responded to Innocent's pitch. Simmons quotes Pinto as saying, "I agreed to read the business plan. The premise was that the U.S. market demonstrated that there was a serious market for smoothies. The argument was that this was transferable to the UK. In the UK, there was only PJ's, but the belief was that the product was not really up to snuff. However, they had established a useful beachhead so we could piggyback in on that by attacking with a better product."

Pinto had recognized the market for *better*. Not bigger, not cheaper: *better*, the bedrock of the NEO Economy. Had the company attracted Traditional capital it would likely have gone in a completely different direction. In Pinto, without realizing it, a NEO company, had found a NEO backer. Now Innocent could reach out to the UK's approximately 12 million NEOs and 11 million Evolvers without compromising or pulling back from the edge.

In contrast, the tension between the founding vision and the reality of corporate expectations that followed PJ's acquisition by Pepsi echoed the tensions that arose within Apple when Pepsi-pedigreed John Scully was at the helm. His values and experience told him to pull Apple over towards Planet Traditional and focus upon the brand rather than the authenticity of the product, just as Walmart-trained Bill Donald did at Starbucks, removing the extraordinary and unique in favor of cost-savings and simplicity of operation. When the PJ's brand didn't live up to Pepsi's expectations it did the predictable thing: worked even harder on branding and promotion. Every move it made allowed Innocent to outflank PJ's by appealing more to the core drivers of the NEOs and Evolvers. And without these customers, PJ's was doomed.

The Innocent founders' approach was "Make 100% natural, delicious, healthy stuff, 100% of the time" and "Do it better than anyone else." When they went to suppliers they ran into exactly the same problem as Harry Cragoe had. But they didn't yield. The suppliers all told them they had to use concentrate, stabilizers, or add sugar. But the team from Innocent kept asking, "Why?" To every unwelcome, negative response they asked "Why?" again, until eventually the suppliers conceded that what they were asking for was possible after all. They chipped away at the objections until they got their own way. It was this unrelenting unwillingness to compromise that pushed Innocent ahead of PJ's and all other potential rivals, and set the scene for its huge success.

In *A Book about Innocent,* co-founder Richard Reed and Head of Creative Dan Germain wrote, "...we had to find a way to make ours a better alternative to PJ's. To do so, our approach was simple; we'd make ours the natural way." PJs' compromise decision to make its smoothies from concentrates, made in turn from low-quality fruit juice, was coming back to haunt it. Initially it made the business easier and even, for a while, more profitable. But ultimately, the compromise in taste and nutritional value left PJ's vulnerable. Innocent was about to expand the outer boundaries of the market, pushing PJ's back in to the middle ground of being neither extraordinary nor the extraordinary deal, and in doing so, sealing its fate.

As it happens, PJ's did ultimately buy its own plant and began manufacturing its own drinks. This would have been a golden opportunity to make the switch from concentrate to fresh fruit pulp, giving the company the opportunity to reclaim the lead. Instead, it stuck with the concentrate. It was, at this point, successful, it had built a strong brand and, using Traditional logic, there was nothing to justify increasing the cost base of the product. You just don't do that in Traditional capitalism. These seemingly sound business decisions were creating fatal vulnerabilities and value mismatches with the customers. Without knowing about NEOs and Traditionals, PJ's was creating the path to its own destruction.

Innocent was clever in its use of the internet, building an appealing site, and sending out a newsletter which rapidly reached a circulation of 100,000. This enabled the company to effectively engage with NEOs spread across the UK. And when the NEOs did engage, there was a great story to tell about how the company started and how authentic the product was.

NEOs value authenticity highly. Authenticity is about being who you are, not who you should be. If you try to present yourself as something you're not, and your NEO customers find out, you'll lose them as soon as they spot an alternative they regard as the real deal.

The fact that PJ's had built a brand around two people who didn't exist left the company vulnerable in a way it could never have imagined. After all, it was just following a strategy that had long proved successful for other companies, including Betty Crocker and Aunt Jemima. But this established and accepted Traditional approach jars with NEOs' desire for authenticity. And the internet had just made it much easier for NEOs to look beyond the marketing and seek out the truth about who they wanted to buy from. As journalist David Teather wrote about PJ's, "...the brand never had the offbeat credentials that it would have liked buyers to believe."

It's not the concept of branding itself that's under question here, its how you go about the process, what lies behind the brand and which direction it takes you in—Planet NEO or Planet Traditional. Unfortunately, despite Harry Cragoe's passion for the product he wanted to launch, the fictitious back-story of PJ's threw his company out of alignment with NEOs at a time when the Virtuous Cycle made congruence increasingly important--and when a direct competitor, Innocent, had a compelling a story to tell. Like massive armies throughout history which have been defeated by more nimble foe, he was outflanked.

Traditional approaches to branding emphasize the importance of brand attributes. In Cragoe's own words, PJ's wanted to be a fun brand. In their values document, Innocent's founders wanted to 'have fun.' At first blush, these two aims sound synonymous, but NEOs quickly used dozens of tiny clues (the result of hundreds of tiny decisions, each one seemingly inconsequential) to bring very different meanings to the way these aims were realized.

Innocent designed its vans to look like cows, and they soon became a familiar sight around the streets of west London, home to the head office, 'Fruit Towers.' A sense of fun and playfulness permeated every aspect of the company behind the scenes, from the floor covering (Astro-Turf rather than carpet) to the job titles (Queen Bee and Chief Squeezer being just two examples). The accounts of those who work there indicate that the offices have the same kind of high-energy campus feel associated with other companies that evoke fierce loyalty, such as Google. It's no surprise that Innocent was quickly voted one of the best places to work in the UK. That, in turn, increased the number of people who wanted to work at the company, and specifically made it easier to recruit people who shared a NEO worldview, driving the company further forward and further away from the opposition. 'Having fun' had become a competitive advantage.

But if you make 'fun' integral to who you are, you have to find a way of letting the people who buy your product have fun, as well as your employees. And again, Innocent delivered. The company launched its own music festival, Fruitstock, and later took to running Summer Fetes. Simmons quotes an Innocent fan known only as Sage as saying, "Innocent labels claim that 'if you're bored' you can call them for a chat--a big difference to the stark 'Freephone Customer Careline 1-800 DONT BOTHER' message found on a can of Coca-Cola." The number provided goes through to what Innocent refers to as the 'banana phone,' and it is always answered. If anyone calls around Christmas, they are likely to have carols sung to them. One "Drinker" (Innocent's preferred name for its customers) who called the banana phone invited the staffer who answered to come to a party--and was amazed when a group of people from the company turned up, bearing smoothies. In a move that would horrify many Traditional executives, 'Drinkers' are invited to pop into the company's offices when they are in the neighborhood. It's a genuine offer that is honored with charming hospitality as various people (including journalists dropping by anonymously) have attested.

Like many companies, including PJ's, Innocent placed great importance on its labels. In this case, the labels quickly evolved into a place for absurdist humor (listing traffic cones as ingredients) and cheeky jokes ("Lost Property. We found all these after our Fruitstock Festival in August--a set of house keys, a pair of reading specs, a few pairs of sunglasses and a pretty dress. If any of them belong to you, please ring the banana phone as soon as possible, as all of it technically becomes ours in three months time and Jon is really looking forward to getting his hands on the dress.") This irreverence and informality wasn't an artificial construct dreamed up as part of the branding strategy. It was at the heart of the company's culture and as such it was a natural fit with NEO identity and values.

The way the issue of price was handled at Innocent versus PJ's is also revealing. Harry Cragoe showed some sensitivity around the subject. In a 2008 interview in UK business magazine *Management Today*, he spoke about PJ's decision to launch a children's range, saying, "Frooties still contain 100% fruit, but they're not as thick as a smoothie and they're smaller, so they are cheaper to buy. It means that you can buy a healthy drink for your kids that isn't packed full of synthetic sugars and isn't as expensive as other smoothies." At Innocent there was no apologizing for the cost.

In his book, Simmons writes, "If Innocent gets criticized, it is usually on the grounds of price. 'Your stuff's really expensive' is the most common complaint." But he also notes, "the founders had an exceptionally clear idea of the typical Innocent consumer: themselves...and they can afford to pay £1.80 ($3) or more for a 250ml bottle of a juice drink." In the same way that they were immovable on quality, right from the start Innocent's decision-makers were firm in their belief that people would pay a premium for what they were offering. They were right.

The company's stance on environmental issues was also a perfect fit with its NEO customers. It used recycled material in its plastic bottles, sourced fruit approved by the Rain Forest Alliance and, in 2004, set up the Innocent Foundation, which gives grants and "works with NGOs to deliver our vision of sustainable farming for a secure future." In the past two decades or so, many companies have tried to incorporate similar green and ethical virtues into their business model. But despite talk about the 'triple bottom line,' they often struggle to give a strong business case for these initiatives, making them vulnerable to any cost-cutting accountant with a red pen. In many cases, the accountants are correct in their assertion that customers don't want to pay extra--Traditional consumers generally don't. But for Innocent's founders, this approach was just a natural offshoot of their own authentic values. They happened to be in perfect alignment with the values held by many of their customers. Had they been selling commoditized big-box juices through supermarket chains, they would have met a very different response.

But just as the company seemed to have created an unassailable position on Planet NEO, things started to get challenging. First, Innocent trialed its smoothies in McDonald's Happy Meals through 80 outlets in England's northeast. The worldwide web is a natural gathering point for NEOs; previously this had worked to the company's huge advantage, now the blogosphere went wild with accusations of selling out. Co-founderRichard Reed defended the decision, denying the charge, and arguing that the company was doing something to ensure that kids had a healthy element in their fast food meals.

But the furor caused by the company's involvement with McDonald's was nothing compared to what was to come. Coca Cola took a 20 percent stake in the business in 2009, and then in 2010 increased this to a 58 percent stake, in a deal worth an estimated £75m ($115m). Ever alert for hypocrisy or inauthenticity, NEOs were quick to voice the opinion that Innocent had lost its unique selling point and become "just another unethical company." Indeed, some bloggers speculated that perhaps they'd been "played" all along in "yet another marketing game" and insisted the only appropriate response was a boycott.

Again, Reed was quick to speak out, pointing out that founders had sold their own shares in order to give Coke its 58 percent stake; that this sale would let them continue to direct the company and its growth; and that Coke would be 'passive investor'. Not everyone was convinced by this, although 30 or more people who had posted furious messages on the company's website were astounded when Reed personally contacted them to present his case.

The loss of those customers who cannot bear to buy anything associated with McDonald's or Coca Cola may be offset by the increase in sales afforded by the growth in distribution, but decisions like this leave the companies that make them vulnerable to being outflanked by what NEOs perceive as a better alternative coming along. Just as Innocent outflanked PJ's, the company that had almost singlehandedly created a smoothie market in the UK, it too could easily be rendered irrelevant by a competitor with a high-quality product whose values are more closely aligned with NEO consumers.

The consequences of a mismatch between company and capital is a vital point that must be considered not just by those running successful NEO businesses, but also by takeover or equity capital investors. No matter how good they look on paper, such deals will only work if investors can, a) secure the long-term participation of the people who founded the company and therefore established its culture, and b) leave those founders free to explore the new opportunities afforded without dreaded "integration" crushing the very thing that made the business attractive to investment in the first place.

The more you examine these culture clashes and the impact they've had on companies as diverse as Apple, Starbucks, and PJ's, the more obvious it becomes that we need a whole new way of doing things. In order to keep building the NEO Economy and to seize all of opportunities within it, we need a new approach to capital. We need capital that can maximize the value of a company by recognizing the importance of its being unique, individual and irreplaceable. In other words, capital that eschews the rules of the Traditional model. The 'build a company, sell it and hang around on a consulting contract just until they tell you to leave and let the new guys run it' approach has killed off more potentially great businesses than anything else.

The demise of PJ's shows how quickly the edge can move, and how calamitous it is to find the ground has shifted beneath your feet. Being a NEO yourself and starting a business based on genuine passion isn't enough to protect you from the misery of a failed company if you don't have authenticity and uniqueness on your side, and if you don't make decisions that keep pushing that edge outwards. The things that make a NEO business extraordinary and authentic should be so much a part of the company's DNA that they can't be replicated. The moment you accept compromises or take shortcuts is the moment you allow a competitor to do what you do but, do it better.

As noted earlier, it was the development of the mass market and the culture of commoditization that allowed NEOs' presence to be felt: they had something to react against, and that allowed them to differentiate themselves as a group. In the past few chapters we've looked at the perils of bringing a commoditized approach to a NEO business. But the process can work in reverse, and work brilliantly.

There are already a number of businesses that have cleverly stepped in and transformed something that has been commoditized into something that is unique and extraordinary, and they've found tremendous success doing it. But the potential still awaiting others able to do this is enormous. And so are the financial rewards. Here is the scope to build businesses that will provide economic growth, high value employment and sustainability, and that will stay in America, since moving them somewhere else would rip out the very heart of what makes them successful. By aligning customers, companies, and a new kind of capital, we can not only create the extra growth that America needs right now, we can actually future-proof our economy.

At first, this might seem all too hard. Trying to de-commoditize might seem as futile as trying to turn back the tide. But that's not so. In fact, to begin to see the possibilities, think about the service you get in your dozens of daily transactions. Good, personalized service has been one of the biggest casualties of the drive towards commoditization. Most of us regularly experience service so frustratingly bad that phrases like 'call center' are shorthand for a sour joke.

No one enjoys it, but Traditionals are willing to put up with this slide to lousy service if it saves the bottom-line. NEOs are different—again, for them, commercial transactions are often about experience, not just acquisition. And if you get the experience right, they will reward you.

One company that has found the truth of this is Zappos, and its story is all about how to do things right and reap the rewards.

CHAPTER EIGHT
SUCCESS AND THE SIX-HOUR
CUSTOMER CALL

Innovation. It is such an appealing word, full of promise. It seems to offer solutions to all the problems of today; a route to a better tomorrow. Every day we hear calls for innovation, and the more the economy is challenged, the more urgently we're told that businesses, employees, scientists, educators, markets, government and even children must innovate if we are to compete globally in the 21st century.

But what does this really mean?

If you are able to ignore the hyperbole and speech-making for long enough, you'll notice that innovation is already all around us. In fact, it is the source of many of the structural problems our country faces today.

The technological innovations of the past few years that were once amazing are now so commonplace we often don't even recognize them for what they are. What might once have been a mind-blowing leap forward is now "just another upgrade." The dot.com era has given way to social media and 'the cloud,' revolutionizing the way we connect with one another and further ingraining technology into our daily lives. Some of the changes wrought by these innovations improve lives. But some do the opposite. When a team of warehouse managers is replaced by a handheld tracking device that instantly uploads data on product status, delivery, and shelf-life that, too, is innovation. But it doesn't necessarily make America a better place to live.

Many workers are with that team of warehouse managers now out of work, locked in an unwinnable competition with computer chips. When an assistant loses their job because a scheduling program has been developed to allow executives to manage their own time, or a bank teller is let go because fewer and fewer people actually come in to the branch, they're not falling to others willing to work for less somewhere in the developing world. Instead, they have been replaced by circuitry, and the innovation that lies behind it.

We're witness to a growing mismatch between the skills of the workforce we have today and the one we need for tomorrow. Like many western economies, we face severe structural problems that came to a head in 2008, after growing for decades. The increasing economic divide between the technically proficient and those who lack the necessary skills (and the subsequent downward spiral of the middle class) can be blamed, at least in part, on innovation.

Part of the response needed lies, of course, in our education system. But that's a medium- to long-term strategy. In the meantime, we are left with a problem that we need to deal with now. It's a human problem that cannot simply be wished away. Macro economics is important, but it's hard to care about that on the micro scale: the growth of high-tech engineering jobs in Cupertino isn't much comfort to you if you lost your construction job in Florida when the housing bubble burst.

Even "a life-long commitment to upgrading skills" isn't a panacea. It sounds like a good plan (and it is certainly vastly better than making no attempt to progress) but as fast as retraining programs for workers can be implemented, technology is moving even faster. And it's often moving in directions those designing the skills training could not anticipate. Take, for example, the huge amount of time, energy, and money invested by individuals and companies over recent years in learning and improving their own data storage, customer-management, and communication systems, only to see them made redundant by cloud-based innovations that require different knowledge and skills.

Nor is innovation just about computing progress. Every time a company takes advantage of the opportunities of an international supply chain, that too is innovation. Changing the way a company manufactures, so that its microwave ovens are produced not in Andover, Massachusetts, but in a state of the art factory in China's Guangdong Province is the very definition of innovation: a new method, a new approach. It's just not the kind of warm-glow, saving-our-future newness that use of the word generally implies.

This is not an argument against innovation. That would be absurd and fruitless. Innovation is as much of a given as the rising of the sun or the movement of the tides. But in order to be able to think usefully about the kind of innovation that will improve the American economy, and American lives, we need to be able to recognize that innovation simply means change, and that change can be for the better or for the worse.

The Two Planet prism is an incredibly useful tool for examining the quality of innovation, and being able to determine whether specific innovations will produce higher levels of domestic employment, demand and satisfaction...or not. This knowledge leads to the next step: putting resources into creating those innovations which suddenly reveal the kind of "magical demand" that appeared in response to the iPad. What may seem, at first, like a mysterious, alchemical reaction when, say, an authentic restaurant opens in a NEO neighborhood and draws queues around the block every night, is in fact predictable. Knowing how and why it works mean we can unleash this kind of demand right across the NEO Economy, and elevate the entire country with it.

One essential element in any valuable NEO transaction is personal connection and service. Sounds almost old-fashioned, doesn't it? Compare the number of staff in an Apple store to that in a Staples. Innovations in technology have given Traditional companies in all kinds of commoditized industries the ability to 'manage' us customers more efficiently. This means viewing us as account numbers and funneling virtually all communication through 'customer contact centers.' When the process began, these centers were staffed with people who shared your time zone, if not your zip code. The development of web-enabled and voice-activated services replaced many of those jobs, and those that were left got pushed ever further away, consolidated into massive call centers in places like Vancouver, BC and Halifax, Nova Scotia, where Canadians at least sounded more like Americans. Finally, they went offshore, primarily to the Indian subcontinent, where young men and women with advanced degrees answer the phones using assumed American accents and names.

The Traditional Economy's relentless pressure to reduce costs and compete on price made this progression inevitable. As a result the real economic value of individualization and personal connection is lost, and ever greater offers are required to bring new customers in the front door faster than the existing ones are leaving out the back. In the process, margins get squeezed and the pressure continues to cut costs and increase efficiency yet again.

Think of the airline industry. What was once the epitome of glamour, with authoritative, dashing pilots and beautiful, elegant air hostesses welcoming well-dressed passengers, is now unrecognizable. Airline travel has, almost completely, become a commodity and its providers compete aggressively on price, brand and features (differentiating themselves by, for instance, magnanimously allowing us to bring along luggage at "no extra cost"). The phrase 'cattle class' used to be half-joking; now it's an accurate description (even for most business travelers).

But before you can board your plane, you need to negotiate the ticket-buying process. If you simply want to fly from A to B, don't especially care what time you travel, and aren't attempting to 'pay' using frequent flyer miles, this can be a reasonably simple online transaction. However, if you need even the smallest amount of extra assistance, information or variation, you'll find yourself in a very particular electronic hell.

Americans are enthusiastic online shoppers. In 2011, according to online tracking company ComScore, our online retail spending was an astronomical $161.5 billion. We get it. We know how it works. Why, then, do so many companies treat any attempt to reach them other than through their websites as evidence of idiocy? Airlines are prime offenders. Call the contact number provided on the website and you're almost guaranteed to be shunted into a loop of recorded messages suggesting you check the website for the answer to your query. This ignores the blindingly obvious fact that if it were possible to solve your problem online, you would have already done so, instead of wasting precious time trying to make it through their phone maze.

We recently experienced this blank incomprehension and refusal to engage while trying to book a domestic flight for an adult and two pre-school children. It surely won't come as a surprise to you that Thomas, the adult in question, wanted to ensure that he and his children were seated together. But this simple requirement proved too hard for a succession of airlines. As a frequent solo business traveler, Thomas just assumed the booking process would be as painless as usual. However, it emerged that his preferred carrier (with whom he has racked up many, many air miles) had no facility for assigning seats for children in advance. Hmm, odd, but surely a call would fix it?

Having persisted through the lengthy and tedious recorded messages urging him to visit the website; he was finally connected with an agent somewhere in the world. A very polite young lady with a clearly inauthentic mid-western accent explained it was not possible to meet his request because it was "against our policy," but if he turned up at the airport early it would "probably be o.k." A supervisor proved equally unhelpful and yet the call ended, as the call center script directed, with a thanks for calling the airline and the reassurance that they appreciated Thomas' business (though he hadn't given them any that day, and was now unlikely to ever do so again).

Two hours and four airlines later, a human being solved the whole problem in just a few minutes. Michael at Alaska Airlines had four young kids of his own and immediately understood what needed to be done. He explained that all airlines have the policy of not pre-seating families, but holding back seats, which are allocated just before the flight. However, he then convinced his supervisor to override the policy and book the seats. It was only after this was done, that our grateful customer realized he had stopped asking about price an hour and a half ago. Getting the *right* deal, not the cheapest deal, was his highest priority. It turned out that getting this highly personalized service cost $45 per seat more than the price of seats on the first airline he'd tried. To many Traditionals, this extra charge would indicate a bargain lost. NEOs see the world differently. For them, it is the cost of having their needs met in a way that competitors flatly declared impossible. As such, it represents excellent value for money.

In the name of containing costs and streamlining operations, billions of dollars in potential earnings simply never reach companies unable to offer the personalized solutions that NEOs seek. Those who do understand the NEO worldview are left with a clear run at all that available expenditure.

Richard Genovese is one such astute entrepreneur. At the Clayquot Wilderness Lodge near Tofino on Vancouver Island, Genovese and his family provide guests from all over the world with beautiful tents equipped with king-sized beds. Each night they sit down with each guest and design the next day's activities so each person gets a highly personalized adventure: learning how to surf on a pristine beach, tracking grizzly bears as they hunt Sockeye salmon in the rushing rivers, or kayaking alongside the orcas that swim around the island. There are no packages, no schedules, and no rules (other than to respect nature). The cost is $1,500 a night, more than any five-star hotel within a thousand miles. It is booked out months in advance.

That's the top end of the market, but the principles Richard Genovese employs can be brought to bear on any business aimed at NEOs, whether it's selling a $4 cup of coffee or an investment account. What Genovese and other like him have done instinctively is to offer something that stands in sharp contrast to the brands and conformity of Traditional Capitalism. In doing so, they have revealed a demand that was lying there, latent, the whole time.

For these business owners, innovation always focuses on uniqueness and experience tailored to individuals. This genuinely NEO approach should not be confused with the cookie-cutter "special" treatment offered by banks and hotel chains and other major corporations. Segmenting their customers by income or purchase patterns, they offer those who they judge to be in the top echelon upgrades, private bankers or other inducements designed to make them feel elite and valued. But two things are wrong with this approach. First, the filters these companies use to identify this group are blunt instruments indeed. In grouping people by income, they mistakenly believe they are revealing those most likely to spend more. Not so. Even previous purchases only show you how people have reacted to the available choices, not how they might react if they were offered a genuine (NEO) alternative. Second, for all that they are presented as "special," these programs take a blanket approach. It's a smaller blanket than that thrown over the company's customers as whole, but it's a blanket nonetheless.

If you want to suddenly reveal hidden levels of demand, create something that appeals to the 59 million NEO "markets of one" and the 54 million Evolvers (they have the same drivers to spend and if you treat them like they matter, they will be yours for life by the time they are fully evolved NEOs). That's precisely what Nick Swinmurn and Tony Hsieh did, creating a billion dollar company and thousands of high quality domestic jobs in the process.

Delivering Happiness

Many successful entrepreneurs begin by spotting a gap in the market. These two did the opposite, finding success in a market so crowded that entering it seemed like folly. By 1999, Tony Hsieh already had a dot.com track record. He had sold his first company, ad network Link Exchange, to Microsoft five years earlier for $265 million. When Nick Swinmurn set out to launch an online shoe retailer (initially called shoestock.com, then renamed Zappos), the dot.com bubble was already bursting, so he brought Hsieh in to help. Even with his impressive pedigree, Hsieh struggled to reverse the tide and attract the additional funding to create the big online brand he envisaged.

Hsieh believed major brand presence was necessary because there isn't anything innovative about selling shoes: they were widely available, including at discount- and high-margin retailers. Worse, they were seen as being particularly ill suited to the online environment--it's notoriously hard to know how a shoe will fit until you actually try it on. Tricky to do via a browser.

The lack of available capital meant that Hsieh couldn't do what he planned to do, follow the Traditional playbook and spend lots of money on brand building. Instead, he decided to use what money he had to get the best awareness bang for his buck. Hsieh focused intensely on search-engine marketing. Anyone looking for shoes online would find Zappos.

That was a good start, but it was the insight Hsieh had next, and its perfect alignment with NEOs, that would create an extraordinary success: a company with revenue of more than $1 billion by 2008. Less than two years after that, Amazon bought Zappos for more than $1.2 billion dollars (and protected their investment by agreeing to let CEO Hsieh and his team to continue to run it exactly the way they wanted to).

At the time Zappos launched, other catalogue suppliers, both on- and off line, were competing on a mixture of brand and deal in a race towards the bottom. Hsieh knew he could never win this race. He also had faced the fact that there was no possibility of Zappos being able to stand out or create a point of difference by *what* it sold. So, in a stroke of genius, Hsieh decided to put the emphasis on *how* they sold. Zappos would become the best company to deal with, offering the best customer service. Not good service or even very good. The best.

One crucial element of delivering this was the recognition that many of the shoes the company shipped would ultimately be returned. Rather than do the Traditional thing and see that as a nuisance for the company which would translate into a burden for the customers, Zappos embraced it.

From the start, Zappos paid shipping costs—and, where possible, arranged overnight delivery, surprising and delighting customers who were expecting to have to wait much longer. Its return policy was all in favor of the customer: you could send the shoes back at anytime within 365 days of purchase, and Zappos would pay for that shipping, too. Any time a customer wanted to phone, there was always a real person at the end of the line and they were glad to talk to you.

Hsieh had come to the firm belief that the road to success lay in the connections Zappos could build with customers. He thought of this as "delivering happiness" (later using the phrase as the title of his book about the company). When people made an order, he and his team weren't just delivering shoes, they were delivering an experience, they were creating an emotion."Customer care" is a much misused term. Hsieh showed how genuinely it could be meant. Instead of regarding the care of his customers as a cost overhead to be controlled and minimalized, Hsieh made it the heart of the business. And he imbued every single employee with this philosophy, so the person at the end of the line swam into focus as an individual, not an account number or an order. With this simple, yet profound, approach Zappos built genuine relationships with its customers.

As sincere as Hsieh's intentions were, they would probably have come to naught if he'd followed the Traditional approach and spelled out the rules of customer care in thick policy manuals. Airlines, banks, cable companies...they all have these manuals and, as we all know, any customer deviation from the script brings it all crashing down like a house of cards. Instead of writing manuals, Hsieh did something radical. He decided to trust his employees. Setting just a few inviolate rules, he let the staff be the judge of what was going to best deliver happiness to the individual customer they were dealing with.

One shining example of what happened next was reported by *Inc. Magazine*: A customer called to arrange the return of an order that had been made by her husband, who had subsequently died in a car accident. The return was arranged, and the next day the customer received a bouquet of flowers and a personal note from the Zappos staffer who had taken her call. She had used her initiative, charging the flowers to the company without even needing a supervisor to sign off on it. If you've got this far into the book without being able to figure out if you're a NEO or a Traditional, your reaction to this story will probably make it clear. Traditionals tend to regard the staffer's actions as playing dangerously free with company money. For NEOs it was the right and human thing to do. NEOs with an interest in psychology might also point out that it is highly effective public relations.

Edward L. Bernays, considered by many to be the father of modern public relations, explained the craft as devising strategies that go against the normal flow of events, things that disrupt familiar sequences in order to attract attention and create an impression. In short, we notice what is different. Commoditization has made lousy customer service normal. To be given individual attention by someone who is determined to solve our problems and deliver us a little happiness is different. It makes us feel good, and it's so rare it makes us sit up and take notice.

What Hsieh did was to effectively remove any barriers that would prevent his people from offering this the kind of extraordinary service.

As unpleasant as it is to be the customer in the average call-center encounter, spare a thought for those on the other side. People who have worked in call centers tell of being under immense pressure to process each call as quickly as possible in order to meet targets they had no hand in setting. Their responses are bound by the options laid out in the manual, with no tolerance for variation. Even with the best will in the world, their hands are tied. There is no possibility of establishing a common understanding. It is pure transaction.

Zappos staff work under no such constraints. They have explicit freedom to delight and amaze. Hsieh reports with a kind of pride that one call saw an agent on the phone with a customer for six hours. "What if they were all like this?" cry Traditional managers, flinging their hands up in horror. Working on instinct and common sense, Hsieh knew they wouldn't be.

Within a short time, 75 percent of Zappos' transactions were repeat customers. Its new purchasers were attracted by what others were saying about the company on- and off line. Social media was the perfect tool to fuel the company's growth, led by customers. Zappos is one of the most followed brands on Twitter, but never uses the service to make offers. Rather, its tweets attempt to give followers an insight to what makes the company unique and the culture that drives it.

Of course, to create and sustain this excellence of experience you have to have the right people. Here, once again Zappos rewrote the rulebook. The company selects its customer service staff not so much on the basis of resume or qualifications, but on their synergy with company values. Specifically, it seeks people who are outgoing, helpful and in general possession of personality characteristics and traits that make them good 'brand ambassadors'. These sought-after characteristics are not the typical corporate ones; they include including 'being humble' and 'creating a little weirdness'. It's also company practice that no matter what role you are hired for, you start in the customer contact center. If you want to be part of Zappos, you have to experience its heart.

Zappos certainly isn't the first or only company to have done this, with Southwest Airlines being perhaps the most well known. But Hsieh introduced one more, highly unusual step. After each employee has been hired and put through the training program, they are offered cash to leave. As the company became more successful the amounts offered went up and up, eventually equating to months of work. Some take it, but the vast majority don't. For Hsieh, those who stay are indicating they are aligned with the Zappos core values, not just marking time in a job. Again, to many traditional personnel managers, this approach seems perverse. In fact, it is highly economical compared to the amount of time and recruitment-and training dollars lost to staff turnover in the average company.

As with other entrepreneurs whose businesses we have analyzed, Tony Hsieh was a NEO who, without realizing it in these terms, created a company in perfect alignment with others like him. NEOs gravitate to companies which give them the ability to exert control over their time by being able to buy 24/7 (being nine times more likely to be heavy internet users than Traditionals). As we know, they also rate the experience of the transaction highly. So while initially people would have found Zappos after searching for terms such as 'platform shoes' or 'brogues' or brands such as Manolo Blahnik, once they arrived they received a service that made them want to come back.

The irreverent and informal culture of the company that came through loud and clear was also a natural fit for the less status- and less rule-based NEOs and Evolvers (and as with Innocent Smoothies, this wasn't something grafted on to appeal to a certain type of person, it was genuine.) When a NEO consumer 'falls in love' it's because they feel they are seeing the heart and soul of a company, not the brand. The Zappos' customer center is in Las Vegas. If you're ever in town, go and visit it and take one of its tours to see this culture in action.

NEOs and Evolvers are 176 percent more likely to refer products, services, and people to others than Traditionals are. Happy NEO customers recruit others, who do the same in turn. This is creates a sustainable business advantage because it means you can save significantly on advertising and the other costs involved in acquiring customers--much of the work is being done for you.

Zappos is selling a commodity, shoes. But by basing itself firmly on the NEO Planet (where much of life is lived online) and making each transaction a unique experience (thanks to that extraordinary service) it has shown how even if you're in the commodity business, you can become an enormous NEO success. And because the company's biggest asset is its ability to relate to its customers, there is no way Zappos could ever be moved offshore or replaced with the latest computer chip: the authenticity would be lost. The American jobs it has created are future-proofed.

This can't be reverse-engineered. You can't simply shift jobs back onshore and then try to charge people extra. The product *or service* has to be extraordinary in the first place. 'Local' is nice but it's not enough for NEOs. Being treated as an individual is what's "worth it" to these consumers; the companies which can do this are the ones they will reward with their business. Our research is clear on the fact that service is important to Traditionals too; if you ask them they will tell you that they want it to be better. But crucially, they are far less willing to pay more for it. For them, it's not a deal-breaker. If you are a business targeting Traditionals, you need to aim for a balance of good service and maintain a competitive price. But if it comes to the crunch and something has to give, focus on price above service.

For NEOs the approach is very different. They don't want to hear about solutions "for people like you," or solutions "for people with similar problems." They want a real connection and they want a solution to their own, specific problem. Opportunities are rife for those able to recognize that innovation doesn't have to be about developing new products, you can also innovate in the way you build the connection with your customers.

The Zappos story is noteworthy. But what's truly remarkable is how many untapped opportunities there are to match its success. There are potential new business models in virtually every part of the economy. There is no Zappos equivalent among the banks, airlines, insurance companies, car rental agencies, healthcare, and on and on. But the customers who value the Zappos approach have bank accounts, travel frequently, rent cars often, and buy insurance, healthcare, and thousands of other products.

Those 59 million people have the financial capacity and the proven willingness to pay for the unique, personal, and individual. But in so many areas right now they aren't being offered that, so the demand remains hidden and goes unfulfilled. If the price point allows, this potential market swells up to 113 million Americans, and this is mirrored in advanced consumer societies across the globe.

NEOs are the renewable energy source that can fuel the fire of the American economy. There is an endless debate in economic circles about how to increase 'Aggregate Demand,' with opposing views deadlocked into a standoff of lower taxation versus spending. But there is another way. Tony Hsieh and thousands of other entrepreneurs are already showing how it can be done, even if they don't yet use the language of the Two Planets.

For every company that wants to succeed in the NEO Economy, the challenge is to put in place processes and staff to build a true connection with the most important people in business, your NEO customers. The bigger you get, the more thought you need to put in to how you can act small, in other words, how you can behave quickly and flexibly when presented with a real time individual need.

To do this, you'll need to create channels so that your customers can tell you what they want, and you can take note. But, as we saw with Starbucks' customer feedback experience, you need the tools to differentiate feedback. There are no average consumers. NEOs and Traditionals want, and will pay for, very different things. You need to know how to channel the NEOs because they are the co-creators in your business model. The opportunities in the Neo Economy are vast but you're going to need a new rulebook.

CHAPTER NINE
"WORTH IT"

This new rulebook is all about understanding the difference in the meaning of the word "value" on each of the Two Planets. By now the potential of the NEO Economy should be crystal clear. It's a game changer on the biggest scale. As we've seen, it won't be built by producing homogenized goods and services at lower and lower cost, but instead by providing things that can be made here and represent "good value" in the eyes of people willing to pay for them.

For those who don't yet understand the Two Planet Principle, "good value"—in other words the idea of something being "worth it" or "not worth it" —seems like an arbitrary judgment. In fact, as we know, it is the bottom-line expression of core values. These distinct sets of core values are what separate NEOs from Traditionals. The two groups may use the same words when they talk about value, but they are speaking different languages. As the Two Planet Principle becomes integral to your way of seeing what is going on around you, so does your ability to correctly predict what will be seen as good value by each group, and what won't.

Stuck as they are in the old frameworks, most commentators haven't noticed that there is a difference in the meaning of 'value,' so what hope is there that they can see how it might translate to the wider economy? Take, for example, online discount engines such as Groupon and Living Social. They have become business-media pin-ups because of their ability to generate huge sales volumes. Living Social proudly trumpeted its achievement in selling more than one million Amazon.com gift cards in less than 24 hours, and many reporters joined the applause. The cards, worth $20 each, sold for $10.

As far as the two planets are concerned, NEOs are 91 percent more likely to use Groupon than a Traditional because they are the ones more heavily on line and are ruthlessly able to use every tool available to take advantage of lower prices once they find something they like.

It's unsurprising that they snapped the cards up, as the product was purely a commodity. But what we find remarkable is that the ability to sell something for half price is seen as noteworthy. Hasn't it always been easy to swap a $20 bill for a $10 one?

There's no argument that these companies provide local retailers with access to a market way beyond their normal reach, but ultimately they are another brick in the wall of increased commoditization. The focus is always on price; that's their purpose for existing, hence the collective name, deal-of-the-day websites. Groupon's advertising has always emphasized this, using a tongue-in-cheek approach that went wrong in one of its 2011 Superbowl ads.

The ads featured various celebrities promoting what seemed to be worthy "Save the ..." causes (Elizabeth Hurley on Brazilian rainforests; Cuba Gooding Jr. on whales) but then revealed themselves to be discounts on things such as Brazilian waxes or whale-watching tours, in keeping with the company's 'Save the Money' slogan.

However the version which opened with actor Timothy Hutton speaking somberly about "the people of Tibet" whose "very culture is in jeopardy," then cut to him sitting in a Tibetan restaurant in Chicago bragging about scoring a $30 fish curry for half price didn't go down well. Social media was aflame with condemnation and, despite having Greenpeace on its side, ("since it began as a collective action and philanthropy site..." read the statement from Greenpeace, to which people can donate through Groupon), the company acknowledged that it had gone too far and pulled the ad. It might have been a joke that went wrong, but the ad was completely upfront. The message was 'it's all about the price and we can get you the lowest one'. Which it often can.

Groupon has users from both planets. As we have observed, when something is a commodity and the only differential is price, NEO and Traditional behavior is virtually identical: they both look for the best deal. Nobody wants to pay more for something than they have to. However, while deep discounting can be a useful marketing tactic for moving excess inventory or attracting people to a slow night in a restaurant, it strips away a business's ability to distinguish itself on any basis *other* than price. That's a much bigger loss than most participants realize. They are sacrificing their chance to be recognized as the kind of "high value" business whose profits underpin the NEO Economy. Notice you haven't seen any Apple, Patagonia, or Anthropologie coupons recently.

Many retailers have entered a state of almost perma-discounting in a desperate attempt to attract customers. Stroll into many Macy's stores on a non-sales day and you're likely to have the place almost to yourself. As with many other retailers, it has to constantly tempt purchasers into its stores with offer after offer and one sales event after another. Like it or not, what was once "America's store" is now all about the deal. Why? Many will tell you that it is the "bad economy," but it is far more fundamental than that and will last long beyond the next swing of the trade cycle. Just as for many auto companies, airlines, hotels, chain restaurants and countless other stores and products, its offerings have become de facto commodities; so it is entirely predictable that price, features and status drive sales numbers, as that is what is driving their customers.

The executives of these companies report "increased competitive pressure" and the need to deepen discounts and raise incentives to retain market share. Management is trained to pivot in these circumstances, as Macy's has, to be able to still make money in this new reality, but it does so primarily by cutting costs and often increasingly driving the company ever more in to a less differentiated, commoditized trap. This means fewer staff, lower wages, and benefits over time for those who've kept their jobs, and the squeezing of suppliers to maintain margins. Those suppliers squeeze the next guy down the line, who then replaces people with machines or other, cheaper people, and the downward cycle continues, with an impact that rips at the very heart of the American middle class.

The downward pressure on prices is relentless. Many consumers have technology in their hands that would have been science fiction just a decade ago. If you have a smartphone, you have the ability to hunt down the best deal. And nobody's playing nice. In a June 2011 article in the Small Business section of *The New York Times*, the owner of Kopp's Cycle in Princeton, New Jersey, Charles Kuhn, described his new reality: "People come in with their smartphone and scan a barcode on a product that I have in my showroom, and what comes up on the phone is the three closest places and their price and then also what [it would cost purchased from] Amazon."

This means that to succeed in the commoditized atmosphere of Planet Traditional you need to engage in deal extremism. Canadian furniture retailer The Brick understands this perfectly. The company doesn't try to tell you about the quality of its designs or the thickness of the leather on its couches, it just rolls from sales event to sales event with a relentless energy that can only be admired. The Warehouse Sale is followed by the Valentine's Day sale, then the Tent Sale and endless other variations. And these are real deals, not just hype.

Of course the margins are small, but the volume is high, and increasingly the company is making a greater proportion of its profits from financing. We'll let you guess how much of the product is made in North America versus how many manufacturing jobs it has created in China, but The Brick is delivering precisely what Planet Traditional wants and needs.

Of course as their income and wealth levels grow, Traditionals will shop for different kinds of things. But their purchasing decisions are still made through the same prism: a combination of price, features and status. There are 10.4 million people (4.1% of the population) who are High Status Traditionals; they're the ones who dominate fields such as finance, medicine and real estate development and are the executives of many of the major companies.

For many of these High Status Traditionals, spending is often "conspicuous," it is a way of expressing their separation from others who are less successful. So big houses are just visible through big gates, cars are either loud and ostentatious or large and distinct, and trinkets are plentiful. Brands matter a lot. The archduke of this realm is Donald Trump, who insists that everything he has is "the best, the biggest" and often the boldest. But Trump always prides himself on getting the best deal when he is spending his own money.

One High Status Traditional client of ours, who is very wealthy and enjoys a fabulous lifestyle of private planes, luxury homes, and fast cars, stayed recently at a major hotel in Las Vegas. He knew they had condos for sale and that the market there was awful, so he asked the brokers how much for the penthouse? Quoted the list price of $12 million, he pulled out his checkbook and handed them a check for $1million, saying, "I'm leaving on Monday, let me know if you are going to cash it." Did he really want the penthouse? Of course not. But he couldn't resist the chance to try to score a great deal.

With wealth inequality growing across the globe there is increased focus upon a tiny fraction of people with incredible means--often called the 1%. These people seem, to many companies, to behold a safe haven of economic support as their wealth is almost untouchable. However, a look beneath the surface shows that even within that wealth bracket the Neo and Traditional drivers still hold. During the worst of the economic crisis media was full of "wealthy" people "doing with less" and shunning conspicuous consumption, with a massive impact upon many of the highest status brands on the planet. These were exactly the same reactions as lower income Traditionals were feeling, as spending money felt wholly unsafe to them at the time. Our research shows that similarly wealthy NEOs returned to their pre-crash spending levels months ahead of Traditionals, however, as even at the highest levels, wealth remained an incredibly poor indicator of propensity to spend.

As stock markets recovered, the wealthiest Traditionals, who hold a far higher percentage of their wealth in financial instruments, started to feel safe once again and spending returned. The rapid pick up of sales at high end retailers and many of the highest status products highlighted an increasing divide between the richest and the rest in the country and have become a social point for demonstrations and argument. What gets lost in all of this is what is really driving the 52% of the population that are Traditionals--safety. Lower income Traditionals hold a much higher percentage of their wealth in their primary asset: their home.

This was, of course, the same asset class that had driven so much spending in the preceding boom, as housing prices seemed to soar on forever, but was subsequently devastated as the system of financial instruments that poured cash into the real estate market unwound in a hurry. The popping of the real estate bubble and the destruction of millions of jobs founded upon the consumption driven by the illusion of wealth created by the "safe" asset of housing has put many Traditionals into a tailspin that could go on for years. The important thing to understand is that, for Traditionals, a huge proportion of the population, there will be no recovery in spending to drive the economy until they feel safe. The Catch 22 of all this, of course, is that, in an economy reliant upon consumer spending, recovery is challenging without their participation. To rebuild the U.S. economy, we are going to have to have a NEO revolution.

Many of the ideas commonly held about 'luxury' are clearly Planet Traditional concepts. Even though status is at the heart of the offering, this leads to risky thinking. If you're targeting High Status Traditionals, do you really want to be the third most covetable brand in Swiss watches, luxury hotels, or sports cars? It's a slippery slope to competing solely on price, and the slide down is awfully steep.

More fundamentally, how good a business strategy is it to go after that market of 10.4 million and in the process alienate yourself from the NEO and Evolver market of 113 million, who care about very different things? Companies such as Apple, Innocent Smoothies, Zappos, Anthropologie, and Lululemon have succeeded by doing the diametric opposite. They created goods and services that appealed to NEOs and Evolvers. Occasionally, and once they were considered "safe," the Traditionals even followed!

Design, provenance, individuality, personal relationship, and authenticity: these are among the key factors that drive NEOs to make very different decisions than Traditionals. They don't preclude a NEO buying something that might be regarded as by others a high status luxury brand. They're just buying for a different reason than the Traditional at the next counter. If a wealthy NEO loves the feel of a Mont Blanc pen or the sound a Mercedes Benz coupe makes as it accelerates, they will happily buy them. In both cases, it is the personal meaning, connection, and experience of the products, rather than its status, features, or even price that motivates them.

For NEOs, "worth it" means that whatever purchase they are considering fits a matrix of values that is far broader and individualistic than the Traditional criteria. It would be wrong to say price is irrelevant, but it is just one factor they will consider. As we've seen with previous examples, once they have decided they want

something, NEOs will then use all of tools at their fingertips to find the best price.

Yvon Chouinard and Eric Skokan are two men who have instinctively understood what's "worth it" on Planet NEO all the way through the process, from the germ of an idea to the paying of the bill. They don't know one other, and their businesses are very different—so different that if you don't understand the Two Planet Principle you wouldn't even spot the core values that mean they have many more similarities than differences. Let us explain.

Yvon Chouinard started and runs a company whose brand has become iconic. Eric Skokan operates in a completely different, much more local sphere. But each has become successful by appealing to other people who share their own definition of "worth it."

Chouinard's company is Patagonia. It began in the mid-1960s when he and a few friends started making and selling climbing equipment they had developed as an alternative to the available tools, which they'd seen damage rock faces. In his book *Let My People Go Surfing*, Chouinard explains, "None of us saw the business as an end in itself. It was just a way to pay the bills so we could go off on climbing trips."

Nevertheless, word began to spread amongst the climbing community, and sales grew until Chouinard Equipment supplied more climbing equipment than any other company in the United States. Profitability, however, remained at the very margin because the company was constantly evolving its designs, an expensive endeavor as it meant continually retooling for the new lines it was introducing.

The first catalogue, issued in 1972, opened with a lengthy essay on the environmental virtues of 'clean climbing,' i.e., using equipment that minimized the environmental damage caused by the sport. Nowadays that might seem like a very mainstream, even obvious position. But it was far from widely accepted at the time. Right from the start, Chouinard provided his potential customers with a rich and thoughtful back-story and aligned his company with a clear set of values.

In due course, the company sold off the climbing equipment part of its operations and turned its focus to Patagonia, Inc., supplying clothing and gear for sports ranging from fly-fishing to surfing, and pursuits such as yoga. But it upheld its commitment to the environment by financially supporting environmental causes and by carefully examining every step in its production processes to ensure that each is sustainable. When it did identify any problems, it quickly addressed them. As a result, many commentators have suggested that Patagonia's success is due to its image as a 'green' company at a time when to be green is hip, ignoring the fact that the company was successful when the idea of 'green' and 'hip' in the same sentence was laughable. (Anyone who swallows this misinformed interpretation and thinks they can tack eco-friendliness on to a business is bound for grave disappointment.)

In reality, Patagonia's success is due to a number of factors that meant the company was inherently, if unknowingly, set up to find the very edge of Planet NEO and stay there.

To begin with, there is Chouinard himself. Charismatic, charming, daring, visionary, and, of course a superb climber, he has a twinkle in his eyes that seems to say that were you, by some freak twist of fate, snowed into a remote cabin together at Thanksgiving, he'd still be holding you enthralled with his stories by spring. You also get the impression that even in his mid-seventies, as he is, he'd have all the skills and ability needed to have kept you alive in the meantime. All businesses are started by someone, but on Planet NEO it sure helps if that someone is so totally captivating, clearly a passionate and a nice guy to boot.

Then there are the products. The gear that established Chouinard Equipment was unique and so authentic that it not only changed the way people climbed, it was part of the movement that helped change the way people viewed the environment. The company didn't adopt an environmental policy because it was the hot thing to do (it wasn't). It was simply a natural expression of the way Chouinard and his collaborators felt. That's never changed and now its given voice through environmental reports and essays on the company's website, written not by the marketing department, but by people out there in the field. Literally.

The company keeps itself at the edge by constantly developing new lines and products, and ensuring each one exists for a purpose. The gear might look great and be favored by 'weekend warriors,' but it has to work. If you are setting out to climb K2, nicknamed the Savage Mountain because of it claims the lives of one in four of those who have tried to scale it, you want to know that your clothing is going to stop you from freezing to death, not that it is available in this season's colors.

It's also made to endure. As one user, Paul A. from Oakland, commented on the customer-reviews site Yelp.com, "7/23/2010 In February, I bought a pair of khakis from Patagonia and since then I have put them through the ringer. I have taken them through the snow and granite of South Lake Tahoe, the volcanic basalt...of Table Mountain/Gold Wall in Sonora and the wind and rain of Mt. St. Helena in Calistoga, CA. Each test I put them through they passed with flying colors. I highly recommend Patagonia products. Yes Patagonia products are expensive (hence the moniker Patagucci-dubbed by the Yuppies) but well worth the price.'

The company's hiring policy also helps it maintain its alignment with customers by preferring 'people who love to spend as much time as possible in the mountains or in the wild'. Chouinard says, 'All the better if they have excellent qualifications for whatever job we hire them for, but we'll often take a risk on an itinerant rock climber that we wouldn't on a run-of-the-mill MBA.' Unsurprisingly, this has a direct benefit for customers who can get advice from sales staff who know and love the same sport in a way that is impossible to fake or half bake.

NEOs and Evolvers feel a connection to the company because of this authenticity and because of the 'human' response they get when they make contact. Another Yelp review, this time from Steve T., in Austin, Texas: "I used to drive all the way from Berkeley to Reno to go here (combined with kayaking at the whitewater park, or on the south fork on the way)...The staff is always very helpful and friendly. Once, when I flew in from Austin in the dead of winter and the airline lost my bag, in which all my winter clothing was packed, I drove to the Patagonia store since I had nothing else to do...When the staff saw me walk into the store in a t-shirt, shorts, and Chacos in January, they commented on my cold tolerance. When I explained, they went running all over the place, digging up things they had that they couldn't sell for various and sundry reasons, and GAVE them to me, even though I kept telling them it was alright and I would survive until the next day when my bag arrived."

'Authenticity' doesn't contain a prescription about what you *should* be. It just says, be who you are. All of Chouinard's charisma would be of limited use to him were he selling something he didn't believe in. In other words, if you wanted to get into the outdoor clothing market, you couldn't hope to compete with Patagonia by sending your sales team on weekend team-building workshops in the great outdoors if that wasn't their natural habitat. It might seem glaringly obvious but it is worth repeating: the key thing about authenticity is that you can't fake it.

For Patagonia this carries over into 'celebrity endorsements.' Typically, these are a complete waste of time with NEOs, who tend to neither believe nor care that celebrity X supposedly uses product Y. (Celebrity campaigns still work well with Traditionals though, adding 'status' to the product). Patagonia's version of celebrities, are people it describes on the company website as 'field testers for our gear and storytellers for our tribe.'

Take writer, climber, and AMGA-certified Rock Guide Majka Burhardt. Listed as 'a nationally ranked skier by age 12' she soon tossed that aside in favor of canoeing in northern Minnesota, Canada, and the Arctic, then added climbing and mountaineering to her resume. Not only that, but she holds a BA in Anthropology from Princeton University. Oh, and she built her own straw-bale house. Burhardt's adventures are real and so provide a real test for the product, meaning that this isn't so much an endorsement of the brand as it is an endorsement of its authenticity.

There is, of course, a degree of truth in the "Pata-gucci" jibe: huge numbers of those who wear the brand are not about to climb K2, or anything at all. Even so, they buy the products because they perceive them as "worth it."

Chouinard's commitment to not compromising on the product is what the company is built upon in the same way that the late Steve Jobs' commitment to design and experience built Apple. This passionate extremism is a mark of the people who occupy the outer edge of Planet NEO. If you are to replicate anything from these iconic companies it has to be an unwillingness to yield to the advice of 'market wisdom'.

The reductionist view of successes like Patagonia suggests that business is a mechanical exercise and if you throw switches X, Y, and Z in order, it will deliver exactly the same result time after time. Real world experience teaches us something different. While it is undoubtedly important to be able represent who you are and what you are trying to achieve to a wider audience, there are plenty of success stories that arise from a commitment to something unique, extraordinary and personal. Eric Skokan's is one such story.

Skokan is a chef, farmer and owner of the Black Cat Farm Bistro in Boulder, Colorado. Far from the fanciest of restaurants, it's located in a side street in a building that previously housed a failed Cold Stone Creamery franchise. But Skokan has taken the concept of a local bistro to its absolute extreme and created somewhere that stands out, even in a town of great restaurants. Authenticity is its defining characteristic.

So committed is he to the concept of fresh ingredients, Skokan has established not one but two of his own organic farms, just outside of town, to ensure that he always has the freshest and best to work with. The Black Cat Farms grows "250 heirloom and heritage varietals." As a result the Bistro's menu changes daily as he and his team only pick what is ripe, and build the menu around that.

As with any extremist Skokan wants to take it further, and this year introduced the Black Cat Farm Community Shares Program. The program is "a weekly share of the farm and restaurant's harvest and a community for those who love food and love to cook." By purchasing a Black Cat Farm share, members get to participate in the inner workings of both parts of the business through visits to the farms and conversations with the farmers and chefs. This enables them to experience the "slow turn of the seasons."

With the economy struggling, unemployment at the highest level in living memory and America's future supposedly on the line as "consumers" hold back from spending, Skokan's share holders are spending between $400 and $750 for 20 weeks' worth of access to a farm and produce when it is in season.

To a Traditional this would seem the furthest thing from luxury, but NEOs and Evolvers see things differently. For plenty of them (not all, of course not all, remember its 113 million markets of one) it has far more appeal than a round of golf and cocktails on the veranda at 'the club'.

What unites Yvon Chouinard and Eric Skokan is their ability to connect with people who value what they do and are willing to pay for it. They have found their success on Planet NEO much as Sam Walton of Walmart and Ray Kroc of McDonald's were able to do on Planet Traditional. Each of these four very different people shared values with the people they built their business for, and did not compromise in any way, shape or form to deliver what they themselves valued.

As NEOs wealth levels increase, they continue to decide if something is "worth it" based on the same matrix they used when they had a fraction of the income. It is still unique experiences, whispered secrets, and personal discoveries they wish to indulge in, rather than the 'luxury' rewards that High Status Traditionals seek.

Small and intimate is far more likely to intrigue the wealthy NEO than a global luxury brand. Looking at travel choices, our research shows us that boutique hotels and those with eclectic designs and highly personal services are far more appealing to NEOs than the global brands that appear in every city. Of all the people who stay at Relais & Chateau Hotels, such as the White Barn Inn in Kennebunkport or the Auberge du Soleil in the Napa Valley, 87% are NEOs and Evolvers. In addition, NEOs are ten times more likely than Traditionals to stay at a W Hotel. Statistics like that don't happen by chance.

It is interesting to see NEO poster child company Apple sometimes described as a 'luxury' brand. Not if you're a NEO, it's not. In an online *Forbes* article, analyst Toni Sacconaghi wrote about a February, 2011, meeting at which he was present, along with then Apple COO Tim Cook, CFO Peter Oppenheimer, and Eddy Cue, VP of Internet Services. Sacconaghi recalls Cook saying that iPhones were just below food and water on Maslow's hierarchy of needs.[1] To a Traditional, that is wild hyperbole or just crazy talk. To a NEO it's only a very slight exaggeration.

In the minds of the people who buy them, Apple devices, Patagonia clothing, or even Black Cat Farm Heritage Tomatoes are not luxuries--they might cost more than other similar products, but they are 'worth it'.

When you understand what truly motivates NEOs, you can know which products and services will be a natural fit for them. Otherwise you're just guessing, blindfolded, or making big assumptions on only partial information.

From the perspective of economic and employment growth, the ability to see what truly represents "worth it" to the significant number of Americans who are both high margin and high volume opens up business models that aren't constrained by the relentless pressure of international or technological competition and lowest production costs.

It means we can develop companies and entire industries whose encounters with their customers are not purely transactional, but instead create both relationships and jobs of real value. Jobs that are not only new and vibrant, but are effectively "future proofed" from the next technological step forward or someone else in the world trying to fight their way out of poverty. Take the unique, personal and individual out of The Black Cat or Patagonia and you may save some costs, but you are very unlikely to still be "worth it."

CHAPTER TEN
THE RULES OF THE GLOBAL ECONOMY, THE BAKED IN JOB AND THE SMALL SOLUTION THAT TACKLES THE BIG PROBLEM

To a great extent, commoditization is the force driving some of the seemingly intractable problems the country is battling today.

In fact, the first rule of the global economy is:

Anything that can be commoditized will be commoditized.

In chapter four we talked at great length about the effects of commoditization as it pulls every industry and business sector in a race towards the bottom, but in a global economy it is almost impossible to resist.

The reality is that any job, product or part of a product that is effectively a commodity faces global competition and the threat of new technology making it obsolete, because nobody is going to pay more for something that is exactly the same as something they can get for less.

As we now know, faced with a commodity product, both NEOs and Traditionals behave in exactly the same way, and demand the best deal. Ultimately, irrespective of any amount of advertising, speeches or bumper stickers, people do what makes the most sense judged according to their own self–interest.

Corporations, too, make decisions based on self-interest (meaning the ability to turn a profit and return money to shareholders). Even Steve Jobs got fired from Apple the first time around when results disappointed the shareholders! Politicians who fight over the tax policies that will "bring American jobs home" are conveniently ignoring the fact that the products concerned are being sold to a global audience, not just Americans. As well as cutting their costs, many US corporations see a move offshore as beneficial because that's where bigger market opportunities are going to be in the years ahead.

The process of commoditization is still in full swing and its reach is growing. It has already wreaked havoc on what were once the industrial centers of America, but increasingly white collar jobs are seen as just as "outsourceable" as blue collar jobs have been for decades. The x-rays of U.S. patients are read by technicians in India over the web. Architects pass their drawings around the world so they can be worked on 24-hours a day by skilled high quality draftsmen in Mumbai, Beijing, and St. Petersburg, delivering work faster and more cheaply for clients.

Virtually every major technology company now has research labs in Asia, not only because that is where the market will be but also because that is where the talent is. It is a myth that jobs are only ever outsourced for lower costs. With foreign universities graduating millions of new engineers, doctors, draftsmen, and every other discipline, each of them hungry and looking to make his or her mark, the pressure is not letting up. In the words of one senior auto executive "in those countries we get someone from the top third of their graduating class, in America it is usually from the bottom third."

Walmart isn't one of the most successful companies in the world today by chance. The people who created the company understood from the very first day the nature of commoditized products. This means Walmart, with its slogan, 'Save Money. Live Better,' appeals to both the huge number of Traditionals, who make their purchase decisions based almost entirely on price, features, and status, *and* to many NEOs and Evolvers who go there to buy things with which they have low personal engagement, meaning they are, in effect, acting just like Traditionals.

The reality is that not only is the reach of commoditization increasing, but its rate is also speeding up. When Apple launched its new iPhone 4S, the big feature was the voice control app, Siri. Apple actually only fully acquired the company behind the Siri technology on the day the service was launched, after it had been under development for four years. It met with a great reception and was seen as a clear differentiator, separating the iPhone from all of its competitors who had recently been bringing out faster, lighter, bigger screen phones, typically at lower prices. However within eight hours of Apple launching this breakthrough piece of technology, IRIS (yes, Siri spelt backward) was launched on the Android store.

This voice-activation software was developed by a small software company in Bangalore, India. Was it as good as Siri? Reviews suggested not, or more precisely, not yet. Nevertheless much of the technological advantage that initially made the iPhone a category of one was wiped out in less than a day. In a globalized world, where products are copied, features duplicated, and brands invented and trashed at tremendous speed, the downward pressure upon prices is immense. To the individual consumer, that comes as a huge benefit. But to the economy at large, it is coming at an ever higher cost.

Some say we have to remove additional costs imposed upon American businesses and squeeze our labor costs, but even if we erode our environmental, labor, and social protections to engage in a race to the bottom, it is a race we cannot win. There is always somewhere that will be able to produce it cheaper or with fewer restrictions. In any race to the bottom, there are very few winners and many losers.

No amount of regulatory relaxation, wage reductions or tax credits can ultimately save us from the next rung down on the ladder of commoditization. If the industrial regions of southern China become more expensive through an improvement in their rewards to labor and international pressure for environmental protections, then the country's western provinces will take over production of the labor heavy jobs. If prices increase there, manufacturers will move on. There are still a great many hungry people in the world prepared to work for next to nothing. Ultimately, once a product is commoditized, everyone ends up competing with the lowest cost producer, whether that is on the other side of town or the other side of the globe.

Commoditization opens up the world to global opportunities but it also opens up the world of global competition. We have to grasp this concept and its consequences if we are to be able to address the deep problems within the U.S. and other Western economies and to build industries, companies and opportunities that actually can recover our economic and financial stature, not just kick the problem down the road through another couple of trade cycles.

But what about the 'Sputnik moment' that President Obama called for in his 2011 State of The Union speech? Could that really be the route out of our current economic problems to prosperity?

While it's certainly true that America's 1950s drive to succeed led to an historic redirection of funds into science and engineering projects, and these projects catapulted America ahead, times have changed too much for as similar investment now to deliver the same results. It will bring benefits, but they will be different benefits.

Six decades later, the motivation that got us into the space race looks a little different than it did at the time--less about glorious exploration and more about a dread fear of falling behind the Soviets. Nonetheless, there were many huge commercial benefits that came as a side-effect of this of this commitment to innovation. Aircraft anti-icing systems, radial tires, Tempur "memory" foam, and pretty much every modern major breakthrough in fire resistance are examples of spin-offs from our original Sputnik moment.

Those developments were more than just great ideas. They became great products and, crucially, products manufactured right here in America.

But times have changed, and we suggest that our generation's Sputnik moment might produce great ideas and products, but the first rule of the global economy —everything that can be commoditized will be commoditized— means that it won't produce American manufacturing jobs. What happened at Evergreen Solar is a great example of why not.

Evergreen Solar is the pre-cursor to Solyndra. This solar technology company built a large manufacturing plant in Massachusetts in 2008, after the state government provided a variety of financial incentives, including grants, tax breaks, and free rent. The company grew and became an all-around success story--one utilizing cutting-edge technology in the politically sexy "green jobs economy" to provide jobs for around 800 people in the area. It was an economic win/win. Then in January 2011, the company announced that it was closing its plant, selling its assets, and relocating production to China.

This news was followed by an inevitable outcry from people who had lost their jobs, and state officials were left explaining why they had used taxpayers' money to grow jobs on American that ended up in China. The right used it as an example of why 'the government' can't pick winners and why it should play no role in trying to establish new industries here. The painful truth is that Evergreen Solar had no choice. Continuing to manufacture here in the USA was only going to drive them out of business.

The company had built a terrific product, slightly better than many of its competitors perhaps, using great engineering, good business management, and a lot of effort from everyone involved from the top to the bottom. In the Hollywood version, this is the point where the end credits would roll and we would all feel good that CEO Ben Affleck had won the day. But the world is a lot more Oliver Stone than many would like to admit.

In reality, Evergreen Solar was in an industry that, despite being "new" and "green," had already become commoditized.

In the global economy, no matter how much you think you have built a better mousetrap, very quickly it just becomes an everyday mousetrap. The features you have worked so hard to create are rapidly incorporated into everyone else's products. In many cases, beyond the intellectual property rights for those who made it, innovation is often no longer a killer app, but just something for everyone else to copy.

Evergreen's issues were not ones of branding, operations, or vision. Selling a commoditized product, it needed to be able to offer the extraordinary deal to win the day; coming in a distant but gallant second was deadly. Evergreen, as with so many other companies, found time and time again that it could not compete based upon anything else *other* than price, making the cost of production the singularly most important part of its business. It had to move production to somewhere cheaper than Massachusetts or it was done for.

It's highly unlikely that technological innovation will create the number of jobs needed. It's worth remembering that Apple has changed the world, but it employs fewer than 47,000 people on American soil.

This brings us to the second rule of the global economy:

You cannot market your way out of a fundamental problem.

Ultimate Electronics filed for bankruptcy in early 2011. From a marketing perspective it had as good a Traditional marketing position as is possible to devise. Their stores' tagline was "If you buy anywhere else, you will have paid too much!" Unfortunately, it just wasn't quite true enough. Aggressive marketing drew customers in to their stores only to find that prices that were pretty much the same as at Best Buy, Costco, and of course the big daddy of the planet, Walmart. There was the odd saving here and there, but not at the "OMG, I can't believe it!" levels that get Traditionals up before dawn on Black Friday. That simply wasn't possible. There wasn't the margin to keep going lower; if the company did so, competitors would just meet the new price and ultimately make business unsustainable.

The company's CEO, Mark Wattles, an extremely bright man whose commitment to the company knew almost no bounds, couldn't overcome the fact that he could only match (not beat) his competitors on price, and with prices set level, most consumers (both NEO and Traditional, since mainstream electronics have been almost completely commoditized) would rather choose one of the larger chains. It was partly status and partly a matter of perceived security: buy a big screen TV and you want to be 100% sure that the company is still around if you need to take it back. Bigger companies seem more likely to last (just don't tell that to the Lehman Brothers stockholders).

If your product is out of alignment with the values of the people it's made for, you will be forced to do whatever you can to get it there. Sometimes there is the chance to go back to the drawing board and come up with something that is genuinely extraordinary, but for most it is a case of having to squeeze margins and drop prices until the existing product becomes the extraordinary deal it should have been in the first place.

A deeper understanding of Planet Traditional also allows us to see the ridiculousness of so many of the arguments put forward by politicians and pundits on both sides of the ideological divide. The U.S. can no more become the lowest-cost producer than it can out-innovate competitors in goods and services that have been reduced to commodities by the oppressive, relentless competition of globalization.

Creating more jobs requiring advanced college degrees is a good idea but is no defense against an increasingly educated and engaged global population or against advances in technology that continually threaten to make skill sets outdated. Neither will it solve the problem of today's pressured middle class. The 45-year-old father-of-three roofing contractor from New Jersey who lost his job when the economy crashed and the 32-year-old single mom from Arizona whose customer service job was replaced by new software are not going to become electrical engineers for Google in California any time soon. However, turning the middle class into the underclass going by paying them less and less isn't going to restore American economic vitality either.

Baked-in jobs

So while it's exciting to talk about a rebirth of American innovation and commitment to entrepreneurship and science, the real question is: are these innovations going to help build a vibrant economy here, or are they just going to lead to more jobs shipped elsewhere in order to thrive?

To put it in Two Planets terminology, are we innovating one-and-only's that simply can't be replicated, or are we innovating commodities?

What we really need is jobs that are not only 'innovated' here but that will stay here and grow; jobs where the very act of outsourcing would remove their meaning and kill their viability. We need non-commoditized jobs in non-commoditized industries. This is the road map for the future of American employment.

That doesn't mean there isn't a future for the commoditized Traditional economy. In fact, our hope is that with a clearer understanding of what really drives the spending of the 52 percent of the population who live on Planet Traditional, businesses orientated towards that part of the market can focus more of their energy on delivering the "extraordinary deal" and less on superbowl ads with rap stars driving cars we all know they wouldn't be seen dead in. Doing so will ensure profitability, which will help our economy. What it won't do is produce a huge number of American jobs.

In an April 2012 article in The Economist, the point was made that digitization of manufacturing could, in effect, lead to some manufacturing being on shore once again, but that it won't be a major job creator, as modern factories rely far more heavily on technology than people, so labor costs are not that big a factor any more. As technology continues to progress, the competition of the American worker is not only with cheaper alternative people around the globe, but robots, who cost the same everywhere. In commodity products, where the lowest price is the key component, we may never see large scale job creation here again.

On Planet NEO, it's a different story. While traditional smoke-stack industries are in decline, other industries are showing signs of incredible growth, even in the face of the economic woes we have experienced over recent years.

It is precisely NEOs and Evolvers revolt against commoditization, along with their willingness to pay more for what they value, that have made many businesses in many sectors thrive despite the wider economic fluctuations. The spending that makes up the NEO Economy has created NEO business success stories. In turn, this creates a different, and considerably more hopeful, future for the American economy--provided we direct our human and capital resources in the right direction.

Sometimes it Takes A Small Solution to Solve A Big Problem

The recent revival of the American craft brewing industry is a clear testament to the power of the NEO Economy.

In 1980 there were fewer than 50 brewers in America. Today, the Brewers Association lists more than 1,600 craft brewers in an industry that employs more than 103,000 people. That's more than a glass half-full. It's the equivalent to almost two and a half new Apples, and it is still growing. More importantly, virtually every one of those jobs is in America, and will never go anywhere else.

Beer sales comprise products from large-scale manufacturers such as Miller and Budweiser; imports such as Corona and Heineken; and beer made by the craft beer industry. The craft industry consists of brewpubs, microbreweries, regional craft breweries, and contract brewing companies (businesses that are hired by another brewery to produce their beer).

In recent times while there has been a year-by-year decrease in beer sales overall, there has been a significant growth in the craft brewing sector. In 2011, for instance, while the Brewers Association reported an overall decrease of 1.2 percent it also noted a remarkable expansion in the craft brewing part of the industry, which grew by 15 percent in that year alone, with more than 250 new breweries opening.

Commentators and analysts have taken notice, but the tools which they are attempting to understand this phenomenon, models developed during the period when Traditionals held economic dominance (The One Planet Economy), are hopelessly inadequate, leading them to miss the real story.

In an article for *Business Week* posted in August 2010, journalist Ben Silverman reported this overall decline in beer sales and the contrasting craft-brewing growth and went on to say that it revealed America's "growing taste for craft beers." He stated, "U.S. beer drinkers want to try new, tasty beers, and they're not dissuaded by the weak economy or higher prices." Silverman quotes C. James Koch, founder and chairman of America's largest craft brewer, Boston Beer, who says, "People have developed a taste for very high-quality, independent brewers," adding, "People are moving out of mass, domestic brands...."

What's wrong with what Silverman and Koch had to say? Surely if sales of craft beers are up then there is an increasing appetite for those beers. That's true, but for everyone who understands the Two Planet Principle it's what's missing from their assessment is the real problem. For us, and we hope, by now for you, alarm bells start sounding when we're told that 'people' are doing this or 'consumers' want that. Which people? Which consumers? Not the millions still happily sipping, gulping or chugging Budweiser, Coors, Miller Lite, or even Heineken, never giving a second thought to the option of a craft beer, and if they did, not prepared to pay the typically higher price for it.

Those seemingly innocuous words "people" and "consumers" sit on a nest of unchallenged assumptions, notably the idea that consumers are all essentially the same; that they act like a herd of skittish wildebeest charging off together in a single direction. It's a variation of the 'everyone is now eating cupcakes' statement that we talked about in chapter one, the kind that only makes sense if you ignore all of those not eating cupcakes.

The danger arises when these kinds of sweeping generalizations becomes the basis for business or economic models. They are the kind of generalizations that can seduce you into no-man's land, the airless void between NEOs and Traditionals where businesses stagnate and often die.

The idea that there is an overall shift in beer consumption, with everyone moving away en masse from mass-produced labels towards craft brews is directly contradicted by our research. In April 2012, we asked our research company to poll our participants about their preferences. Of those asked, three times the number of NEOs preferred craft beer to Traditionals, and seven times the percentage of NEOs had bought or consumed craft beer more than five times in the previous week.

The overall decline in beer sales is due to Traditionals, who have reduced consumption in an entirely predictable response to the contracting economy. But simultaneously NEOs and Evolvers are buying *more* beer. They are, however, buying different beer, and it's the craft beers that fit their tastes and values.

Craft brewers aren't creating this demand, but they are there to meet it (as with many NEO businesses, these brewers are often NEOs themselves, creating a product they would want to consume).

Once you understand the increasing importance of the NEO Economy, the "magical demand" for everything from iPads to IPAs becomes entirely predictable, and can therefore be harnessed for economic regeneration.

In his article Silverman goes on to quote Molson Coors President and Chief Executive Officer, Peter Swinburn, who felt that it would be a "difficult year for the industry" and "the toughest U.S. beer market in decades." Undoubtedly he is right—for his segment of the industry. The mass-produced beer market has become ever more commoditized.

Consumers make their choice on price, status (brand), and features such as packaging or a label that turns blue when it gets cold (it doesn't change the taste, though!). The inevitable consequences of globalization have been one brewery takeover after another, each designed to lower costs, expand brands, and consolidate operations. Today, that classic American beer, Budweiser is, in fact, owned by Brazilian/Belgium conglomerate In-Bev, while Miller turns out its "High-Life" on behalf of its owner, South African Breweries.

While the huge corporations have been doing the belt-tightening and job shedding, craft breweries such as Shipyard Brewing Company in Portland Maine, Avery Brewing in Boulder Colorado, and Sierra Nevada in California have stories of growth and ever greater demand.

But back to Silverman again, and his reference to comments made by market research company, IBIS World's senior industry analyst, George Van Horn. Silverman writes, "Van Horn says the popularity of craft beers reflects an attitude change among U.S. consumers that has played out over several years. Americans are focusing on smaller quantities of food and beverage, but seeking out higher quality, he says, noting that organic food sales have also held up during the downturn." Strangely, in this analysis both Van Horn and Silverman seem to have forgotten the rising rates of obesity in America, the fact that McDonald's is doing just fine during the downturn, and that wine from the "Two Buck Chuck" label Charles Shaw recently turned the commoditized world of table wine on its head. So much for sweeping statements about 'the American consumer'!

Again, one of the key findings of our research is that consumers are remarkably consistent. This applies both to Traditionals, responding to better packaging or buying higher status imported beers over American brands, and to NEOs and Evolvers expressing their individuality and personal values through choosing hand-crafted offerings with which they feel a personal association.   But the polarization of their choices can look like change from a distance.

Silverman wraps up his article thus: "Brewers Association Director, Paul Gatza, additionally attributes the popularity of craft brews to demographic changes, especially the arrival of a new generation of 'Millennials' that doesn't care as much about established brands. 'The beer drinker has changed,' he says. Koch agrees: 'Twenty-Somethings are adopting craft beer in the same way that baby boomers adopted wine.'

This is a great example of what we call PRBA (Partially Right By Accident). Yes, there is a strong representation of younger consumers among the drinkers of craft beers, but it is not their age that guides their choices. Millions of Traditionals who came of age around the millennium are not drinking craft brews; they will happily buy any of the brands they recognize, especially if they are offered an incredible deal. Step into any liquor store on a Friday night and see how many 'Millennials' are walking out with cases of Bud, Miller, or Coors Lite under their arm.

As we have said, demographics are of limited value in the understanding of who is buying what and at what frequency. There are 'Millennial' NEOs and Evolvers just as there are in every other age range category. As Ken Gossman, founder of Sierra Nevada Brewing Co. said as far back as 1999, "We have a pretty broad range of customers. If you go into our restaurant, they are all over the place in terms of age."

The craft brewing industry is almost perfectly in alignment with what NEOs and Evolvers value. The way that the industry talks about itself reads like a checklist of what's important to NEOs, so we're going to reproduce it here with the words that we consider to be the key words picked out in bold. According to the Brewers Association:

- The hallmark of craft beer and craft brewers is **innovation**. Craft brewers **interpret historic styles** with **unique twists** and develop **new styles that have no precedent**.

- .Craft beer is generally made with **traditional ingredients** like malted barley; **interesting** and sometimes **non-traditional** ingredients are often added for **distinctiveness**.

- Craft Brewers tend to be **very involved in their communities** through philanthropy, product donations, volunteerism, and sponsorship of events.

- Craft Brewers have **distinctive, individualistic approaches to connecting with their customers**.

- Craft Brewers **maintain integrity** by what they brew and their general independence, free from a substantial interest by a non-craft brewer.

It's interesting to chart the growth of the craft brewing industry against a very brief history of brewing and the emergency of NEOs and Evolvers as a distinct economic force.

The waves of early immigrants to America brought a taste for beer and the know-how to brew it with them, along with a strong culture of alcohol consumption and the belief (widely held at the time) that it was healthier to drink beer than water. Benjamin Franklin himself is quoted as having said, "Beer is living proof that God loves us and wants to see us happy."

Prior to the industrial revolution, most of the beer consumed in America would have by necessity have come from small, local breweries but this gradually began to change as the process of industrialization became established and transport infrastructure improved. This meant that breweries could produce beer on a much larger scale and distribute it much further. The result was large, robust companies such as Miller Brewing which was founded in 1855 and has survived and prospered despite hurdles such as Prohibition.

Prohibition started in 1920, when laws were passed that banned the sale, manufacture, and transportation of alcohol. This resulted in a huge growth in racketeering and the black market, an increase in crime and enormous social problems. The sheer inability to control what was happening or to police the laws, plus a growing social discontent caused by the Great Depression, meant that the 'noble experiment' (as it was known) was effectively declared a failure, and Prohibition laws were lifted in 1933.

Prohibition forced the closure of many breweries--when it ceased, reportedly fewer than half of the breweries that had existed beforehand reopened. But ironically, it also provided the conditions under which the surviving American brewers were able to prosper. The reduction in the size of the industry resulted in one of the most homogenized brewing styles in the entire world. Because this was a time when Traditionals were in almost complete economic dominance, homogeneity suited the market. Fifty years after prohibition had ended there was no real craft brewing industry to speak of.

Sales figures show that the overall decline in beer sales began around the mid 1980s, but nevertheless by the year 2000, the number of craft breweries had increased to the point where *The American Journal of Sociology* published a paper on the phenomenon.

In 2009, mergers between major mainstream beer companies led to an increase in beer prices just as the country was in recession. Sales dropped 2.2 percent and many retailers feared this decrease would only continue. They were right with sales dropping a further 1.2 percent in 2010 and then again 1.3 percent in 2011.

Let's map this against the emergence of NEOs and Evolvers. As we saw in Chapter Four, various factors needed to be in place to allow NEOs and Evolvers to emerge as a recognizable economic force. It wasn't until the mid- to late-'90s that the combination of technology and demographics allowed drinking-age NEOs to establish themselves as a true economic force. And it was around this time that the micro-brewing industry began to take off.

Sierra Nevada Brewing Co. is one of the biggest successes of craft brewing. Professor Michael J. Lewis of the University of California describes the company as "the most perfect brewing company on the planet" because of its commitment to quality and integrity. The company was founded by Ken Grossman and Paul Camusi. Grossman, a chemistry and physics graduate with a passion for beer, opened the Home Brew Shop in 1976 in Chico, selling equipment and dispensing advice to home brewers.

Home brewing is a hobby that can become a passion, with the potential to drag you into a parallel world where aficionados take an alchemical approach to the pursuit of the perfect brew. Before long, Grossman and Camusi had decided to open their own brewery.

In their own words, they "cobbled together" some "dairy tanks, a soft-drink bottler, and equipment salvaged from defunct breweries to create a microbrewery." They chose the best ingredients, brewed pale ale that is generally agreed amongst beer lovers to be world class and launched The Sierra Nevada Brewing Company in 1980, at a time when most craft brewing was still happening at home in the bath tub!

As is common with NEO companies, demand grew by word of mouth. In 1989, the company opened the Sierra Nevada Taproom and Restaurant, where craft brew beer lovers could go to eat, listen to live music and drink the beer made on site.   This increases the experience of the product, something NEOs and Evolvers are willing to pay for.

Today, the company brews around 700,000 barrels of beer per year and its commitment to not just produce extraordinary brews, but to keep pushing the boundaries while retaining its original values is key. The company doesn't just talk about these values, it acts on them, for instance buying the last active floor hop-roasting plant from the Czech Republic, just to ensure that that art did not disappear completely, or the importing the best hops from New Zealand to ensure that its brews were completely fresh, even in the middle of the Northern hemisphere winter.

There are echoes here of the path trodden by Starbucks. Starbucks began as a single store that sold beans and specialist equipment in the early seventies before Howard Schultz decided he wanted to open a chain of coffee bars that restored the romance of coffee. Grossman and Camusi were either accomplished artisans at the start or perfected their craft as they went along, but either way they had a purely NEO desire to offer something extraordinary and unique with a great story to tell about provenance.

However, unlike Starbucks (and indeed Apple), Sierra Nevada has never faced a change at the helm that has driven the company towards the middle. In 1998, Camusi wanted to sell his shares. This could have meant major breweries attempting to buy into the business (or buy it out), which might have led it into the abyss that PJ's unwittingly fell into when Pepsi bought out the company.

But instead Grossman was able to buy Camusi out and retain control. In an interview in *Modern Brewing Age* Grossman said, "I'm still very much a hands-on brewer, and didn't feel comfortable having a brewery that I didn't have full control over." The result is a brewery that has continued to innovate and thus ensured that even though many other craft brewers have entered the market, it continues to be one of the industry players that define the edge.

The overall decline in beer sales and the growth of the craft brewing industry may continue to change the industry landscape as, inevitably, larger breweries are looking towards the smaller ones and attempting to either adapt or consume what has made them successful. (As Silverman reported, brewery giant Molson Coors, for instance, launched craft brew Blue Moon.) Larger breweries might be able to adopt craft brewing techniques, but they lack the authentic back stories (i.e., provenance) that form an essential part of the NEO business model. Again, from the *Modern Brewery Age* interview, Grossman said, "I think the major brewers can emulate our beers, and certainly brew good quality products. Philosophically, though, I think a lot of our customers want to know that their beer comes from a small family brewery or one that's run by a small group of dedicated people." He may not yet know the terminology, but Ken Grossman could serve as spokesperson for the NEO Economy.

This is a crucial lesson for so many companies that buy smaller more dynamic companies as a hope of capturing "new markets" and "expanding brands." The culture of many of the large corporations in America is inherently Traditional, with an emphasis upon systems, cost management, ROI, and corporate politics.

When they buy NEO companies and try to integrate them, there is a real danger that they will effectively smother the thing that made the company successful and attractive in the first place. Inevitably "experienced" but Traditional management is brought in to "oversee" the new recruit and slowly starts pulling the company away from the NEO edge and dragging it back towards the Traditional side. In many cases, this leads to the company becoming marooned between the two planets, untethered from its original customer base and vulnerable to being outflanked by a newer, more authentic competitor. The same sort of pattern is often seen with angel and venture-capital.

Remember the celebrations that must have gone on behind closed doors when Tropicana bought PJ's? It's often assumed that being bought out by a larger, more established company is the route to success for any fast growth company. But it's not always the case, and it doesn't have to be this way.

Our research shows that the potential of many of these individual NEO companies is much greater than even their founders can envision. While access to capital and distribution continues to rest in Traditional hands, we will continue to see the potential of future equivalents of Apple and Sierra Nevada undercut. Planet NEO needs its own capital, managerial, and investment infrastructure to realize that huge potential--infrastructure that shares the same values as the people not only who start these companies, but the customers who value them.

144

Many NEO Businesses Emerge From the Downward Spiral of Commoditization

The pattern whereby whatever can be commoditized will be commoditized actually creates opportunities: the commoditization of coffee, bread, and beer created the opportunity for Schultz to launch Starbucks, a host of artisan bakers to open their doors, and Sierra Nevada to produce premium products for NEO and Evolver tastes and preferences.

Companies such as Jason's Nut Butters are another great example of this in action. The company creates small batches of peanut, almond, and various other butters with a passionate commitment not only to its own product but also to the community and environment in which it operates. The company's headquarters are solar powered and it pays a premium to have all of the nuts it uses steam pasteurized, rather than use the potentially carcinogenic propylene oxide (PPO) widely used to eradicate the risk of salmonella in almonds. On its website and packaging the sense of authenticity is clear, and clearly not a marketing gimmick. The company openly admits that one of the biggest challenges it faces is in consumer packaging, which is notoriously hard on the environment. So it set a target of at least 33 percent of packaging materials to be made of recycled products by Earth Day.

This is an example of a vibrant NEO alternative to the mainstreaming of one simple category, nut butters. The industry is dominated by major food corporations for whom this is just one of their many brands. In simplistic terms Jason's is the Planet NEO alternative to Jif. Like Apple, Zappos, and even Starbucks in their early days, it is a company built upon a belief that there are other people out there who share their founders' values and will be willing to pay for them.

But the reality is that these companies still need access to distribution. This doesn't mean ending up mid-aisle in every Safeway's across the nation so that Traditionals can shake their heads in disbelief at peanut butter selling for twice the price of the store brand. It means tapping into an entirely different economy which shares its values. This means NEO public relations, NEO marketing, NEO financiers, and a whole host of other skill sets. The NEO Economy and the businesses within it open up opportunities for a whole lot of new NEO suppliers.

The key point however is how the jobs that they create are "future-proofed" as no amount of new technology or lower priced labor can wrench them away, as to do so would go to the very heart of their authenticity and value. Start producing Sierra Nevada Pale Ale in Mexico or Mumbai, or Jason's Nut Butter in Brazil and it becomes just another brand on the shelf or commodity. The NEOs and Evolvers who want the real thing will simply gravitate to the next authentic option.

If the NEO Economy is to fulfill its potential to power us into the next century, however, we must be careful of talking about "small business" in the way others talk about "people" or "consumers."

Most small businesses are small for a reason. They have no ability to grow. They produce a product or service that is basically a local delivery of something that can be produced by many others. They have a role to play, but what we need, overall, is businesses with the ability to grow. That is where the future jobs are.

Understanding what is really driving consumer spending and building on the existing NEO Economy is the first step. But without the ability to direct capital to the right places we will never prosper.

The true Sputnik moment of this generation may well be a NEO moment, as we build an economy based upon our strengths and not our weaknesses, one that can never be outsourced to a third party. But, just as with the first Sputnik moment, it will really all come down to money.

If the money that is made available is directed towards commoditized products, no amount of politics from either side will change the result. On the other hand, if that money is used to boost the NEO economy, we really are building a sustainable future.

The craft brewing story shows how de-commoditization can create high quality jobs right here at home. We're not going to see the return of smokestack industries to American soil, and not everyone is going to become an electrical engineer.

If we start to understand that this really is a consumer economy, and not a corporate economy, and put the focus on where the spending is rather than what businesses are doing, we can follow the NEOs and Evolvers into new and exciting territories. We can create a template for American capital that allows us to unlock the potential of the NEO Economy.

CHAPTER ELEVEN
THE NEXT GREAT ECONOMY

S itting in Boxcar Coffee, we were clearly in a NEO haven. The bustling space was full of people waiting up to six minutes to pay $4 for a cup of coffee where the beans have been ground to order, warmed in a conical vase, and then had ice cubes added just before the point of boiling, to extract the maximum amount of flavor. It was located on a street full of coffee places, yet there was a line out the door.

That was where we had our revelation about all the untapped Neo potential—whole sectors of the economy that were operating purely on Traditional lines. While all of the people around us easily could and did express their individuality in where they drank coffee, what computer they bought, who they bought clothes from and what they ate, every single one of them had a bank account, insurance policies and hundreds of other goods and services for which there was no clear NEO alternative.

With NEOs and Evolvers dominating discretionary spending, there is an extraordinary opportunity to grow our economy on an incremental basis, sustainable over the long term, by increasing the range of offerings they can engage with (and so start behaving like NEOs).

That's what made us realize that NEOs are not only powerful, but they are the answer we have been looking for.

As we said in Chapter One,

An extra one percent of GDP, year after year, derived from increased spending by those with the highest propensity and ability to spend, on top of the economic growth already forecast,

147

turns a slumbering economy into a booming one, shrinks unemployment and allows us to grow out of our debt challenges.

Put simply, a three percent increase in spending by NEOs and Evolvers can lead to a permanent increase in the United States' GDP of one percent. It may take less than a three percent increase, if every dollar spent in the NEO Economy has a higher multiplier effect than a dollar spent in a tollbooth economy.

The nature of our research and the stories we have chosen in order to illustrate it in this book are designed to show you two things:

1. That consumer behaviour is largely predictable once you understand that is not demographics, income or any other single factor that drives spending, but a combination of distinct values, attitudes and behaviours held by the two main groups in society.

2. That the opportunity offered by the NEO Economy is already immense and continues to grow. When Jonathan Ive at Apple designed the iPad, Howard Schultz injected his passion into Starbucks or Tony Hsieh built Zappos to be the most enjoyable company to deal with, they weren't creating the demand for their products or services. The demand was already lying there dormant, with 59 million NEOs and 54 million Evolvers just waiting for someone to create a vessel for their own sense of uniqueness and individuality.

The NEO Economy already exists. Apple is already the world's most valuable company. Zappos is already worth more than a billion dollars. Technology companies such as Facebook and Twitter enable more individualization of the online experience (pity they continue to sell advertising on a basis that has nothing to do with spending!) And Sierra Nevada Brewing Company sees ever more demand for its authentic American Craft beers. By now you'll also recognize other retailers, restaurants and service providers around you which are flourishing despite the supposed "bad economy" and the fact that they don't have the lowest prices.

The Neo Economy is real because NEOs are already here and exerting their influence in all elements of society. By crunching more than two billion data points we have been able to identify an opportunity that is huge in scope and contains the seeds of a much brighter future for the American economy than many would have believed. Against the backdrop of so many industries being torn apart, a new economy is emerging, not *instead* of the old one, but alongside it.

This matters, not just because of what NEOs and Evolvers do now, but because of their as yet unrealized potential. Looking at the "Average American Consumer" leads analysts to believe that everyone is up to their eyeballs in debt, scared of the future and a million miles away from being able to lead an economic recovery. Having made it this far in the book you will know there is no such thing as the "Average American Consumer:" there are Traditionals (including High Status Traditionals) and NEOs (including Evolvers). The Traditionals fit the mold of what we are told about demand in the American economy, but this is far from the whole story.

When commentators talk about the downward spiral of the American economy we need to understand they are only addressing the Traditional Economy. That economy is still with us but it is increasingly being buffeted by relentless global and technological forces. A country like America, with its expectation of a better tomorrow, cannot build its success on the Traditional Economy because it is an area where we have little competitive advantage in a global market.

But America's NEO Economy is made up of 113 million people, who choose to express their individuality in 113 million different ways.

When a businesses "gets them" by producing things which appeal to their core values and drive, they reward it richly. The NEO values, attitudes and behavior are distinct and rarely change. Unlocking the NEO code opens up the chance to drive significant growth in the economy, not temporarily but for good.

Most economists are predicting sluggish growth over the next decade, somewhere in the region of two percent. This will not produce a recovery strong enough to drive significant job growth. The government can't step in; with its debt at record levels, its ability to stimulate the economy is limited by financial as well as political realities. The alternative approach of fiscal austerity, currently being tried across Europe, exacerbates the problems of inadequate demand and stirs up class, ethnic and ideological tensions. We have seen this play out in Europe almost a century ago and must not go down that road again.

We have talked a great deal about how NEOs and Traditionals effectively live on two different planets. Over on Planet NEO, its denizens are optimistic about the future. Research from our research company, Roy Morgan Research, completed in April, 2012, shows that NEOs rated 40 percent higher than Traditionals in measures of consumer confidence. NEOs are also 55 percent more likely than Traditionals to think that they will be financially better off next year and three times more likely to feel good about their own financial economy over the next 12 months. Conversely, Traditionals are 66 percent more likely than NEOs to feel that the next 12 months will be bad for them financially. In other words, irrespective of what may or may not be happening in the economy as a whole, NEOs are confident when they look forward, whilst Traditionals look distinctly fearful.

Taking the U.S. economy from a two percent growth rate to above three percent is enough to change the future for this country. It will produce millions of jobs across a wide array of industries, many of which will be entirely future-proofed and will stay here no matter who invents what new technology or who will work for less overseas. We are at the point where changing the long-term growth curve of the U.S. economy will also change the curve of our future as a society. A vibrant and growing economy creates better options to address the long term problems of the country and the world we live in, no matter what political stripe you are.

So why don't all these NEOs and Evolvers just go out right now and spend that extra three percent and save us all the heartache of long-term economic problems? The answer is ridiculously simple: nobody is offering them anything to spend it on! Psychologists call this "Forced Choice," where people can only choose from the options made available to them. Decisions made purely by looking at consumer behavior through the old prisms, rather than understanding the values and attitudes that drive that behavior, will never reveal what the individual would do when presented with a choice that better suits them.

There were many other tablet computers on the market before Apple introduced the iPad, just as there were plenty of juice options available before Innocent Smoothies turned up on the scene in the UK. However in these and many other examples, demand suddenly appeared for these products as if by magic, driving their exponential success. But it's not magic at all, of course. It was there all along, for those able to recognize what was right before their eyes.

The demand was there, what was lacking was a way for those NEOs, spread across all sorts of demographic groups, to express it. Until it appeared, they cooled their heels and made the best choice they could from the available options. In many cases, where there was nothing to distinguish one product from another other than price, status or features (i.e., it was a commodity) they choose in exactly the way a Traditional chooses all the time. When this happens, NEOs act just like Traditionals, buying on price, features and status--and an opportunity to create the Apple of Banking, the Zappos of Airlines, or the Patagonia of hotels is lost.

The "magical demand" that Neo companies tap into remains hidden in plain view as the "experts" tell us that "everyone" wants the best deal. They deliver this dubious fact while looking right past all the people around them who are using an iPad they paid full retail price for while drinking a beer brewed by somebody they can relate to and wearing a jacket from a company they believe in! Strange world, isn't it?

Right now, a NEO can find a smartphone, coffee shop, and local food source that matches their values, but when it comes to many of the big areas of the economy there simply aren't any NEO choices. Try expressing your individuality when you open a bank account, fly with an airline, hire a car, buy your insurance, or fill a million other everyday needs. Here you'll be met with the featureless wall of corporate conformity, dressed up with a Marketing 101 image that fools no-one. (If only these companies lived the values held dear by the creative's who staff their NEO-heavy advertising agencies we'd be much further along the right path).

So, how do we put all the knowledge of these Two Planets to work to create a sustainable revival within the American economy so it can stand strong against the relentless pressure exerted by both globalization and technology?

Simple, we create more companies that are in line with who the consumers really are.

The NEO Economy is the next great economy, at home and around the world. It can fuel this country for the next 100 years. As yet we do not have the great NEO banks, telcos, automotive, insurance, or power companies. The market for companies of all types and sizes is largely untapped.

The market is also ripe. According to our 2012 research, NEOs are 71 percent more likely than Traditionals to switch banks to one that is more in line with their personal values, 55 percent with insurance companies, and an astounding 92 percent with their Telco provider.

If we embrace products and services designed on NEO principles, not on the lowest price point, we can not only drive job creation and business success at home, we can also make ourselves the leaders in a global economy of high value and high margin customers. The forces that have brought the NEO typology to the fore are not uniquely American. There are more NEOs and more NEO economic clout around this world every day.

You Can't Always Get There From Here

The biggest threat to success in the NEO Economy is moderation. Economic growth and business success comes to those who are most extreme in their alignment with how the consumer decides what to buy. Apple, Patagonia, Anthropologie, Lululemon, Chipotle, and at the other end of the spectrum, Wal-Mart, McDonald's, and Hyundai are all expert at it. In good economic times it's possible to get some short-term success floating between the Two Planets, but when the economy slows or someone comes along who more closely reflects what the consumer truly values (as Innocent did in the UK smoothie market and Starbucks did here), eventually you'll be left gasping for air.

The temptation for business is to see the NEO Economy as something you can capitalize upon once you've learnt some new jargon and put into place some new design. But Microsoft didn't suddenly become Apple just because it opened a series of really nicely laid-out stores and tried to hire "cool people" to work in them. (Where is the Zune today, by the way?) NEOs know the difference between authentic and copies. Who you really are matters.

The other major mistake is to fall back upon single planet thinking and repeat the phrase uttered by executives the world over just before they made the decision that trashed their company: "Look how successful we are being with 24 percent of the population, imagine how successful we will be with 100 percent of it." Kerplunk!

This is why the Two Planet Principle is so important. It's a way of bringing to life not only how deeply distinct NEOs and Traditionals are, but also the vacuum that lies between them. Getting stuck between the NEO desire for the unique, individual, and extraordinary and the Traditional desire for a great deal leaves you with nowhere to go. The best you can hope for in this void is that you'll go out of business quickly so you can go and do something more valuable with your time rather than suffer through a slow and painful exit.

Partially Right is 100 Percent Wrong

Going some of the way and doing some of the things needed to be in alignment with either NEOs or Traditionals is as bad as not even starting. It doesn't matter which planet you choose, if you aren't the real deal you're wasting your time.

Another major mistake is complacency. All the strategy meetings, brainstorming sessions, branding initiatives, focus groups, and past successes in the world won't help if you don't understand your customers better than they understand themselves. In order to stay ahead of the curve you need to give them what they want, even when they can't put into words why they want it. The founders of Apple, Zappos and Innocent understood this because they were creating products and companies they, as NEOs, wanted. They weren't coming up with something that could be marketed to "consumers," "trendsetters," or "people aged 18 to 35." By staying true to their own values, they stumbled across a rich seam of high value, high margin consumers who brought them massive success.

Choose which planet you are on and commit to being an extremist. Push its edge further than anyone else. Let nobody outflank you. NEOs and Traditionals can exist side by side, but two NEO or two Traditional companies trying to sell the same thing to the same group of consumers cannot.

For many of today's corporations this makes life really hard. The reality is that they would need to split themselves into separate

153

groups in order to flourish; each in complete alignment with the people of their chosen Planet. The two groups could still share the commoditized parts of their business, such as accounting, but in culture, personnel, product development, sales, marketing and service they need to be completely separate. We aren't talking different ends of the hallway separate. We are talking different towns, different offices, and different people separate. Failure to do this can only lead to compromise. Compromises are the deadly kryptonite of the Two Planets.

It is cultural issues more than anything else that will hold back many of the major corporations of today. Formed as they were back when Traditional values dominated, they either can't see the need for change or won't make it happen. The net result, however, is that this leaves a huge gap to be filled by new companies, built from the ground up to be part of the NEO Economy, creating growth and millions of new jobs in areas that had previously been seen as stagnant. Social media companies are all very well, but if we want to rebuild the whole American economy we need jobs in banking, insurance, travel, manufacturing, and a whole host of other sectors. Building the NEO versions of these companies and tapping in to the unfulfilled demand of NEOs for the more unique, individual, and authentic will create these jobs.

Every successful NEO company is run by a NEO. Steve Jobs at Apple was just one of the starting points. There's also Chip Wilson at Lululemon, Tony Hseih at Zappos, Glen Senk at Anthropologie, Adam Avery at Avery Brewing Company, Steve Ellis at Chipotle...the list goes on and on. It's not because NEOs necessarily make better CEOs, it's just that you can't give what you don't have. If you yourself don't instantly recognize when something is unique and extraordinary and feel that it is genuinely worth paying more for, what chance do you have of building a business aimed at those who do? All of the people we've named above are really smart operators, but we can say with certainty that if we put them in charge of a Traditional company, all about cost control rather than what's new and innovative, they wouldn't last a year. Authenticity is everything, which is why the NEO Economy will be headed up by NEOs.

The Foundation Characteristics of the NEO Economy

Being a NEO yourself is important if you want to carve a place in the NEO economy, but it's not enough.

Although there are 59 million NEOs and a further 54 million Evolvers, each of them has a strong sense of their own individuality, so you need to start from the principle that each individual is a market of one; anything larger than that and you are missing the point.

The NEO algorithm we have built has been able to isolate the key factors that distinguish NEO consumption from Traditionals, *but also from perceptions of how people are 'expected to behave'*. It looks, and is, complicated in its full form--there are more than 180 characteristics that make up the picture. But, within this there are clear foundation characteristics, the things that are the dominant drivers of NEO behavior and these can be used as a route map for building the NEO Economy. It's a map, not a recipe, because while they have some values in common, NEOs value individualism greatly. To try to find a formula in our analysis would be to replace the flawed constructs of the past with a rigid set of new ideas. Never lose sight of the fact that your goal is to align yourself with the consumer, not to produce a cookie-cutter product that "should" appeal to them.

In the NEO Economy people matter. They matter more than systems, more than technology and more than products. You must flip the business model around and put yourself in the shoes of the customer looking back at you, rather than the usual stance of looking out over a sea of potential customers. This concept is vital.

We are writing this book because we want to make a meaningful contribution to the growth of new businesses, new jobs and opportunities for huge numbers of people. Our goal is to unleash a flood of new products, services, and innovation that delights customers makes a long term contribution to some of the challenges posed by one of the greatest economic shifts since the industrial revolution.

Time, then, for a refresher on the most important people within the NEO Economy: the NEOs and Evolvers themselves.

Chapter Twelve
The New Rules of the New Road

1. Individuality is power

- Individual not corporate; individual responsibility and control; personal relevance not external fads or norms.

2. Personalization outranks customization

- Personal solutions: tailored, idiosyncratic, evolving, engaging.

3. Relationship outranks transaction

- Experience is more important than transaction; relationships, not deals; patience rewarded; shared learning and values.

4. Information is oxygen

- Rich, dense, independent, 24/7; mastery not mass; narrowcast not broadcast.

5. Authenticity is emblematic

- Provenance counts; process is suspect. The story behind everything is important. What you stand for is more important than what you say you've achieved. Actions speak louder than words...but the right words count.

6. The edge is the place to be

- Whispered secrets, outer edges, emerging experiences and ideas, not mainstream, not contrived, NOT fads.

7. Technology accelerates slow time

- Living 24/7, having control of your own time. Swapping fast time for slow time. Choosing to live the way that suits your individual pace. Being open to new ways of doing things (if they deliver the right experience). NOT about the latest gadget but about the latest improvement in "living the way I want to live."

8. Complexity and paradox are seductive

- Able to have more than one persona, more than one career, more than one lifestyle. Slash jobs—"I'm a composer/lawyer." Understanding that the world is not one type of people and one way of living.

9. Change is evolution

- Understanding that progression is rarely linear, and the best experiences are usually not planned.

10. Design is the new Zen

- Experience is all about design: how something feels and makes you feel is just as important as what it's meant to do. Design matters: it reflects highly individualized responses to the world we live in. Good design = good quality. Quality matters in a world where mass production reigns.

1. Individuality is Power

NEOs trust other people and small businesses. They don't trust media, big business, governments or politicians. NEOs insist on individuality. They don't trust institutions that treat them as part of a large group or market segment, and it is this independence, allied with a willingness to pay a premium for it, that makes them so potentially powerful.

NEOs increasingly view institutions in ways that are significantly from Traditionals. Traditionals are much more likely to give what seems to be consent to poor treatment from large institutions because they accept institutional ideals and they don't feel there's much they can do about it. NEOs not only demand better but will move their business to get it, often paying a premium in the process.

As many businesses have grown in scale, the individual has diminished into part of a unit to be managed, handled, or sold to. An unfortunate example of this change comes from home loans: in the past, individual bank managers knew their individual customers and decided about whether they could afford a loan or not. The tick-box approach that replaced those managers resulted in mortgages being issued to customers any real person could have seen had no capacity to service them. Hello, Global Financial Crisis. In a backlash, many people who could afford to buy a home are now being turned down because the automated systems have been tweaked to try to protect the bank from incurring more losses.

Develop a NEO banking alternative and 113 million NEOs and Evolvers will bring their business to it.

2. Personalization Outranks Customization

NEOs insist on making connections that are relevant and intensely personal. If you intend to attract NEOs, you require personalization, not customization.

Providing recommendations based upon other people who are "like you" is not enough for NEOs. It takes time for them to provide personal data to a company that wants them as customers. The type of impersonal, often interrogative, data-gathering corporations conduct in an attempt to achieve customization often has a negative impact on its NEO customers. The corporation treats all customers the same in the first instance and only when they have spent time providing personal details does it begin to treat them differently--this is neither individualization nor personalization.

True personalization does, however, exist both in the physical and the virtual world. Take the local neighborhood where the owners of the Italian restaurant not only recognize you as you come through the door, they know what kind of drink might surprise you and what specials might challenge your taste buds. They do not customize an offering for people like you, they respond to *your* exclusive and distinctive needs. It's what you need and want that matters, rather than what they would like to sell you--and it has to be unexpected, otherwise it's just Traditional predictability. The restaurant owners are attracting high-margin, high-relationship customers and their reward is a long-term high-value partnership.

Understanding this NEO need creates the opportunity for NEO businesses to offer 'user-pays' options that lower the cost-to-serve and increases the margin through a premium for higher degrees of personal attention to the individual NEO. Building products and services that NEO consumers can configure to fit their own individual situation, needs and identity allows NEOs to express their individuality through your product. There is no better example of this than Apple's iPhone. Although there are literally millions of them around the world, all essentially the same from the engineering standpoint, no two have the exact same combination of apps, folders, screensavers, music, videos, and ringtones. As a result, although we both may have an iPhone, this one is definitively "my" iPhone. There is no other one like it.

It is vital however that you do not try to pass off customization as personalization. Just because a user can change a few fields on your web pages does not make it 'personal' for an NEO. Personal means individual, and therefore almost infinitely variable.

3. Relationship Outranks Transaction

NEOs define their style and their lives through relationships. And while a transaction is the goal of the corporation, relationship is the life-blood of the NEO Economy.

Major businesses are interested in taking costs out of the value chain-- creating low-cost channels of sales and distribution. Most of these 'innovations' use customer labor rather than corporate labor. Expertise has been replaced with convenience, but the net result is that the burden of navigating the interaction is increasingly placed upon the customer. Where previously you could speak with a person who did the work, you now have to deal with a computer as you pound away on a touch-tone phone or web page, entering information. Of course there are huge benefits to this in pure transactional instances, but it reduces the interaction to one of a commodity. The moment a customer is seeking something more, the opportunity for a relationship is lost.

Without strong engagement, service and a relationship, a business must compete for each and every transaction--with acquisition costs eight to ten times higher than a business that generates transactions from existing relationships. In addition, many businesses are "churning" their old customers (who have become disenfranchised) out the back door while they are working and spending frantically to bring new customers in the front. This is why understanding the NEO need for more than just a transaction goes right to the bottom line of business.

The personalization of experience that can only be achieved through a real relationship is demonstrably far more important to NEOs than Traditionals. Ploys like the loyalty schemes that almost every company offers these days aren't fooling them. Seen through the Two Planets Principle, it becomes clear that most of these are Traditional commoditized constructs. They offer discounts or rewards in exchange for "loyalty" (not taking your business elsewhere) or for giving up more of your data.

This is not to say transactions are unimportant. Of course they are vital--no one would be in business without them. For high-margin NEO customers, however, the experience and the relationship are more important, and the transaction follows automatically from a successful experience—again and again, as Zappos have proven.

Relationships drive margin because they uncover and motivate higher levels of personalization. NEOs are motivated by, and can rationalize paying more for, something that more closely fits their individual needs and preferences. The opportunities for businesses of all shapes and sizes to create higher value offerings with the built-in flexibility that can only be achieved through human interaction is one of the largest growth engines of new jobs in the NEO Economy.

4. Information is Oxygen

NEOs cherish information and are not overwhelmed by the amount of it available. In fact, NEOs thrive on information. Without information they would be starved of new ideas and perspectives that stimulate and vitalize them and which they constantly use to redefine who they are. To an NEO, information is a shortcut to experience.

NEOs are the individuals who, at any stage in history, will be seeking out new frontiers. They are the explorers of the physical world and of the virtual world. They are willing to try new food, new cultures, and new technology but, first and foremost, they need good information. Because information provides a pathway through complexity, it also reduces the risk of a bad experience and is therefore a critical link to new experiences. This thirst for information is not just for facts, but also for exploration.

Typically, this exploration occurs through a combination of NEOs' real-life experiences and their vicarious experiences through books, magazines and movies. NEOs read voraciously. Indeed, they have the highest level of book and magazine consumption in the world—up to four times more than anyone else. Many people read to lose themselves. NEOs read to find themselves.

NEOs are at the forefront of the personalization of the media. For these high-value individuals, the various mass media have become irrelevant. A variety of sources on the internet provides a faster, more flexible, more relevant source of ideas and information for NEOs. Where old-fashioned media is fixed in time and therefore dates accordingly, digital media including blogs and social media evolves constantly--by the minute rather than by the week or month.

Businesses can unlock customer value from NEOs if they understand that communicating relevant information is essential. To create a high-value relationship with an NEO, transactions must move to the background and experience to the foreground. This requires the use of excellent information in the physical world and outstanding content on the internet.

Online, relevant and engaging content is as important to NEOs as relevant and engaging products. The same is true of the physical world. Rather than just seeing yourself in the business of selling products and services, you need to broaden your scope to realize opportunities to create communities of common interest. This means you don't get to be the sole arbiter of what is right or wrong, bad or good: something which can be a major challenge for those who see themselves defending their company against invaders of their "brand standards."

Perhaps the perfect example of rich authentic content is YELP. For a NEO it is informational nirvana, as it helps them sift through vast numbers of options to find new choices and create the opportunity for new discoveries. Not all information needs to be positive; in fact NEOs are more than likely to be fascinated by lower-starred reviews, especially if most of the others are raves. Finding reviews of a restaurant that complains about one-off events, such as a noisy people at the next table, will not deter a NEO unless that drawback is mentioned again and again. Similarly, finding out that most of the negative comments are from people complaining about price or the quantity of food, as opposed to the quality, might be exactly what the discerning NEO needs to convince them to try it!

5. Authenticity is Emblematic

NEOs seek the genuine article; NEOs seek genuine experiences. The need for authenticity stems from a lack of trust in institutions and corporations and the disappointments we, as a society, have experienced over time from the actions or inactions of these institutions and corporations. The NEO response to this is a need for something and someone to trust that is the polar opposite of disposable products and disposable truths.

The internet has redefined the term disposable with literature, music, and visual art not only being freely available online, but also being created exclusively for the internet. These art forms can be found in seconds, consumed in minutes, and discarded immediately. In this increasingly ephemeral world, NEOs are seeking authentic experiences. They insist on lives filled with change and evolution, and this makes their determination to contrast their mobility with the permanent and the handmade even more significant.

For NEOs, experiences also need to be authentic as the world becomes more fake. Theme parks with a contrived or stage-managed experience have replaced authentic fairgrounds. The ubiquitous food court in the local shopping mall offers inauthentic takes on cuisines of the world, at the expense of the cafes and bistros that used to be nearby. NEOs can see straight through the simulacrums.

The demand for authenticity provides great opportunities for businesses that are run by people with an ethical position. The environment, health, and ethics are significantly more important to NEOs in making purchasing decisions than they are to Traditionals, where they tend to be relegated to the level of another feature, if they are valued at all. But a word of warning: NEOs can detect a fraud from a mile away and they are unforgiving once misled. It is not enough to *talk* about ethical issues. They must permeate every aspect of the enterprise, as they do at Patagonia or that little French patisserie that makes the perfect pain au chocolat rather than a Jumbo Chocolate Croissant the size of your head.

It is this kind of authenticity that NEOs will reward with their high-value business. NEOs see themselves as authentic--they do what they believe and they say what they believe--and they want that reflected in the world around them. They wear their honesty like a badge of honor and expect the enterprises they do business with to do the same. (This makes them challenging for existing businesses that have not been built from the ground up.) Authenticity provides a genuine opportunity for business, because in the NEO Economy authenticity is emblematic.

6. The Edge is the Place To Be

NEOs tend to be ambitious, enjoy hard physical activity, aspire to own things that are better than they have now, and gain a thrill from taking risks. NEOs are constantly on the lookout for new ideas and edgy experiences.

Comfort and familiarity do not attract NEOs, who have a taste for the new and an urge for the edge. Their personal ambition compels them to create new challenges and also motivates them to set and achieve objective, personal milestones. NEOs have a great capacity to achieve, and a need to constantly challenge themselves intellectually and physically. We are all confronted by personal challenges, but NEOs tend to not only cherish them, they construct challenges that test their mettle. These serve as tools for their ongoing self-definition.

NEOs break rules. They question established norms and take them right to the edge. They question everything. Why should they enter personal details more than once? Why should they wait more than one hour for a check to clear? Why can't they have their internet connected at the time that suits them? 'Why are you charging me more for this when it really is no extra cost to you?'

NEO enterprises understand that their customers are a diverse range of individuals who have different needs and preferences, and consequently establish a relationship in which there are a minimum number of rules and where the individual's preferences are respected and valued. NEOs respond well to such a relationship because it is edgy, challenging, and not always predictable. As NEOs are constantly evolving, so must the businesses that they do business with. The NEO customer today will evolve significantly over the coming years, so the businesses that want to serve them have to be geared to keep up.

7. Technology Accelerates Slow Time

NEOs use technology to shift time--from slow time to fast time and back again. Slow time is a luxury when it's truly yours--when you control and cherish it. Slow time regenerates, comforts, and heals. Whether it's filled by a meal, music, reading, or just walking, slow time supports the spirit and reminds us that the world we know is built on foundations that we might otherwise forget in the rush of everyday life. Velocity is necessary and even cherished in the NEO Economy, but slow time takes our souls to another place, a necessary place. Slow time for a NEO tends to be a time when they can explore new possibilities.

Captive time passes slowly too, but it's not the same as slow time because it's not yours to spend as you wish the way you choose to spend it. Being stuck in a traffic jam, or being caught on hold in a phone queue, when you would rather be anywhere else—that's captive time. Because NEOs understand and value slow time, they arrange things accordingly. They use technology shift time to their advantage, accelerating slow time and jettisoning 'captive time' tasks that are mundane and time-consuming.

They are willing to pay for things that accelerate time. If washing the car is a chore, NEOs prefer to pay someone else to do it, freeing time to do something more interesting and challenging. (Of course, it is also entirely possible that some NEOs consider car-washing a therapeutic and satisfying use of slow time.) The slow-time/fast-time trade-off is not designed to "save time." Rather, it allows NEOs to juggle time to suit their priorities and interests. It is a mistake to assume that NEOs are time-poor. NEOs like to be busy, but will always make time for important and satisfying experiences.

Many Traditionals, on the other hand, find the notion of paying someone else to wash their car a complete absurdity when they can do it themselves. Traditionals tend to fill slow time with tasks and don't choose to pay someone else to perform activities they can do themselves. They have no concept of fast time, largely because they don't value experience ahead of transaction.

Businesses which understand the value of time to NEOs and use that knowledge to enable their NEO customers to concentrate on the challenging and edgy aspects of life, not the mundane, will flourish.

8. Complexity and Paradox are Seductive

For NEOs, modern life is <u>not</u> too complicated. They find it easy to understand new concepts and information. They are not worried about science and technology's role in the future and are constantly on the lookout for new technological ideas. NEOs are comfortable with complexity and paradox, partly because they have the capacity to deal with it and partly because it excites them to be able to 'surf' complexity--never really knowing whether they will ride the wave or be dumped.

NEOs also have the skill to decode complexity. This ability applies in every walk of life. In their jobs they need to be constantly challenged or they easily become bored. When they shop they dislike the order and simplicity of the mall and value the complexity and disarray of the neighborhood shopping street. When they go online they are in their element. After all, nothing in our lives is more complex than the worldwide web.

NEOs are also comfortable with fragmentation, which means they can maintain deep and rich involvement in several different areas of interest simultaneously. Fragmentation also means one person can carry several different personas for different situations without feeling any tension between the very different behaviors required. One practical example is the recent phenomenon in the labor market of the 'slash job,' a shorthand term for a person with occupational fragmentation—'I'm a dancer/day trader/landscape gardener'. Handling paradox is a very postmodern skill and it turns on its head the more Traditional approach to product development and marketing. NEOs, who want to be treated as individuals rather than being pigeonholed as a predictable group, can behave in ways that are counter-intuitive. They do not want their behavior to be predictable, so they will often fly in the face of conventional wisdom.

NEOs drink three times as much premium wine than anyone else. They drink expensive wine more regularly, not only in celebration, but because they can. They mark the passage of the day with interesting food and embellish it with interesting wine and they love making a personal connection with the winemaker to create a personal symbol. Wine allows NEOs to connect with themselves, with people they know, and with the place it has come from. The paradox is that although NEOs are more capable than anyone else to consume conspicuously, they often choose inconspicuous consumption. This goes for cars, clothing labels, and restaurants, too. High-value NEOs drink working-class beer in public and expensive, quality wines in private.

This apparently paradoxical behavior, and NEOs' core capability to deal with and decode complexity, means that traditional marketing rules must be abandoned. Repetitive, simple messages highlighting the brand and product are invisible to NEOs. It can be summed up in a single phrase:

"Stop yelling at me, I can't hear what you are saying"

The lessons for business are endless and easily applicable. If you are in business for Traditionals make it clear, simple, and branded. If, on the other hand, your relationship is with NEOs, make it opaque, complex, intelligent, and brand-light (they'll discover who's behind it and love you for not being obvious). Remember, to NEOs, complexity and paradox are seductive.

It is this insight that gives small start-up or artisan businesses as much opportunity to succeed in the NEO Economy as major corporations. To the NEO consumer, having to uncover and work their way through something is not a hurdle but an opportunity for exploration. Learning the detail of how a product is made and why it uses one process and not another can be intoxicating. NEOs love listening to Jonathon Ive, the head of design at Apple, waxing lyrical about the decisions that went into crafting a laptop out of a single piece of aluminum or making a screen a little brighter and more defined than the last model. It feeds their desire and ability to understand products and services beyond the superficial standard business communications.

At Monmouth Coffee Company near Covent Garden in London, the owner Anita Le Roy will spend hours talking to customers about the differences between not only beans and roasts, but the people who grow them. In describing how the practices differ between Ethiopia and Central America and differ again from Indonesia, making you sample cups all the while, she is delivering a rich narrative, not just a hot drink. The whole experience is intoxicating and complex and leaves you with a greater appreciation of the world around you.

9. Change is Evolution

NEOs aspire to own things that are better than what they have now. They are spenders not savers, and buy luxuries. Not luxuries as others may perceive them in terms of high status goods, but things that have a strong personal meaning. When NEOs see something they like they often buy it on impulse and, for many, style and authenticity are more important than price. NEOs are not only comfortable with change-- they actively create it.

However, for NEOs, change must be an evolution. It is a shortcut to the future rather than something to be distrusted about the present. A NEO enterprise must evolve with its NEO customers. The product offering should be reinvented regularly to reflect the changing society. The very look of the space, either physical or online, should change and evolve over time. The challenge is to keep the high-value part of a business moving toward the edge rather than back to the safety of certainty because those very NEOs who are providing the high value are heading towards the edge.

An iconic example of this is Thomas Keller's French Laundry restaurant in the Napa Valley. Of course, as with many fine restaurants the menu changes regularly but it is the appreciation and the way the flow of seasons is embraced and incorporated in to the food that makes the experience continue to evolve. In spring you will be introduced to "English peas, Sacramento Delta Asparagus, and green garlic that are welcomed back like old friends who have stayed away to long." Each time you visit, it feels like the restaurant has moved on and grown a little, so that although it is remarkably consistent in its delivery and execution, each meal strikes you as a totally new experience. Contrast this to the high status Traditional offering at Morton's or The Capital Grille, where consistency is prized over evolution.

Change is a given for NEOs. They are ambitious, strongly aspirational, and they move quickly. But this freedom and velocity should not be confused with consumption promiscuity. As consumers, NEOs are intensely loyal to enterprises that align with their values and expectations and, when they find this, will only move reluctantly.

However, when it comes to their work, they are driven by a personal sense of achievement and more concerned with what they do than where they do it. They tend to be less concerned about security and won't be tied to a job simply for financial gain--they know their worth and know they will be well rewarded elsewhere. This is an unsettling challenge for many employers but it provides a windfall for those employers who are prepared to value and encourage fresh thinking, imagination, and innovation.

The speed at which NEOs change and evolve can also be unsettling for businesses. But the NEO combination of pent-up demand for individual solutions and a willingness to explore new ideas and relationships makes high growth possible for businesses that take on the NEO perspective. NEOs will embrace and reward businesses that provide high value, so any NEO enterprise must have a matching velocity to be able to satisfy them. NEOs are not simple to understand and are not easily engaged. It takes effort and commitment, but it's worth it.

10. Design is the New Zen

How do NEOs come to understand themselves and their place in the world? They relate to the world through design--graphic design, interior design, garden design, architecture, and industrial design. From mobile phones to motor cars, t-shirts to office towers, graphics to typography, design has an impact on how NEOs understand and experience the world. How things look and feel is every bit as important as what they do.

What some commentators have termed the "democratization of design" over the last 20 years--with the makers of everything from household goods to park benches responding to a radical growth in the demand for better design--can now be seen as a natural and predictable effect of the rising importance of NEOs in our society. In a world of mass production, the functional and aesthetic experience of a product is (to NEOs) an ever more valuable and integral part of what makes any product, service or experience differentiated enough to raise it above a mere commodity.

Starwood has been a forerunner in differentiating its hotels through design. It did this first with the W Hotel chain, which sought out distinctive buildings in order to create designs that had individuality and diversity built in. Now the company has taken on the motel experience with the ALOFT brand, rolling out highly distinct and design-centric roadside and airport motels. Using natural materials and high-tech services, it has created a 'designed' experience at the lower end of the price spectrum, focusing on creating enticing public spaces that draw people out of their rooms.

Of course Apple, as ever, does this better than most. While the latest Blackberry, HTC, or Motorola smartphones are incredible pieces of technology, the iPhone remains an individualistic expression of art in the palm of your hand. Without comprehending the value that NEOs place upon design, massive amounts of money get spent by competitors on churning out new products, many with more features, lower prices, and incredible offers, to try and displace the design leader. However these often turn up a few months later in a "buy one get one free" offer while the product with stunning design continues to sell at full retail price. Design matters.

Whatever the business sector, in the NEO Economy it is vital to establish design as one of the core components of your business. Design acts as code, telling NEOS that you understand that details, people, and experiences matter. But it is vital to not confuse design integrity with business integrity. There are very few examples of successful companies which only focus on being at the forefront of design. Most successful companies start with what they stand for, and use design and designers to express these core values. NEOs want to deal with companies which have strong positive values. An ethical stance and the commitment to good design is just a natural extension of this.

Once again we return to the issue of authenticity over superficiality. Don't think that just by hiring an awesome ad agency that produces great creative communications pieces, you can compensate for a badly designed business process. NEOs love design, but not at the cost of a tedious, bureaucratic or time-consuming way of interacting with you. They want the real deal, not fake substitutes. Safeway adding a few isles of organic food displayed on the only recycled wood shelves in the store does not magically turn it into Wholefoods.

Due to their ability to command higher margins, NEO companies tend to attract a lot of attention, not least from competitors. As the insurgents almost universally come at the situation from a product- or service-related perspective, rather than viewing things through the eyes of the consumer, the approach is usually to try to defeat the NEO company on a combination of price, features, and status using heavy advertising or branding. From the Two Planet perspective of course this is doomed, as the only way to defeat the extraordinary is to outflank it with something that is even more extraordinary. So we see Microsoft endlessly and fruitlessly contorting itself to produce consumer products with more features and lower prices than Apple, Nike offering pointless copies of Under Armour, Lincoln trying to out-spec Audi and so on.

NEOs learn through their experiences, and as they gain confidence in their own knowledge they will select a few trusted information sources and an even smaller number of trusted suppliers who can reliably and consistently help them see the 'leading edge.' Then, they want to get more involved, more hands-on. Crossing the experience divide on design has already begun, facilitated by savvy businesses that can see and animate a connection between NEOs and their products and services

The characteristics described in this chapter will come as no surprise to many of the NEOs and Evolvers reading this; they've probably recognized much of themselves in those words. Perhaps only the surprising part to these readers is the sheer number of people who share all or many of their values, since many of the highly individualistic NEOs and Evolvers will have spent their lives bumping up against the mainstream (inherently Traditional) world.

There will always be big corporations, faceless brands and Traditional conformity—there is a massive market for it, with more than 52 percent of the population here in the US and billions more people around the world in the Traditional category. But by embracing the fundamental NEO characteristics, we can build entirely new businesses and expand the reach of those existing ones whose values, attitudes and behaviors are in alignment with them.

The 113 million people who make up the NEO Economy are ready to embrace new companies, products, and people as they flex their growing economic muscle. And the beauty of it is, it doesn't destroy or replace what we already have. Rather, it adds to it in a way that has the capability of creating a thriving economy powerful enough to see America through to the next century.

If you're in business, you should by now be looking at your customers in a completely different way. One which, we hope will be useful to you.

We also hope that we've inspired you to see that there is another way to grow the American economy; one that is based on the idea of doing more of what works.

And if you are a NEO or an Evolver, we hope that you have seen yourself in these pages and now realize the crucial role that you have played in the economy to date and the role that you could play in the future. After all, Steve Jobs may have set out to bring about a revolution and, in the process, created the world's most successful technology company, but he couldn't have done it without you.

About the Authors

Chris Norton

Is the head of the Social Intelligence Group and CEO of Fingerprint Strategies. After working in finance for a number of years he built an espresso business in his native England, despite being told that no one would ever pay $2 for coffee in a paper cup by business experts. He then moved to North America to develop a thriving real estate company by applying the consumer insights that came out of what was then the research behind the Social Intelligence Group. He is also the one who took the discovery of NEOs and turned it into a blueprint for rebuilding the entire American economy and driving change on a massive scale by harnessing the spending power of 113 million people who have been largely misunderstood by businesses, politicians and economists. Lots of people have talked around the NEO Economy, but Chris is the one who put it all together. Chris is difficult, but he is occasionally worth it.

Ross Honeywill

Ross is an internationally published author, social scientist, and acted as a consultant to many household name businesses before developing the algorithm that revealed the existence of NEOs and the NEO Economy. He has previously written three business books, including NEO Power and I-Cons, two narrative non-fiction books and is working on his sixth book, a novel titled Angel's Trumpet. He is currently a doctoral candidate in the School of Philosophy at the University of Tasmania. He is super smart, but never makes you feel stupid.

THE BIG IDEA FUND

The existence of the NEO Economy provides a blueprint for building a sustainable economic engine capable of powering America into the next century. Even though it has already made numerous businesses of all sizes in many sectors successful, there is still tremendous potential for economic growth that can be achieved by providing NEO alternatives across all sectors.

With capital and customers, businesses can't fail. Based on that understanding, Chris Norton set up The Big Idea Fund. A non-profit 501 (3) C Corporation that is wholly owned by its members, the Fund brings together people to generate funds with the aim of taking ownership of or investing in those companies that have the ability to create a sustainable future for America. Members also add their commitment to switching their custom, where relevant to their needs, to those companies the Fund owns or has invested in to guarantee their success. They are the kind of businesses that NEOs and Evolvers already support. The Fund just organizes their capital and puts it to work in a way that creates a world NEOs and Evolvers want to live in.

Find out more at
Thebigidea.org